PANDEMIC PROVERBS 2
More Wisdom for
Troubled Times

by
John
Stanko

urbanpress

Pandemic Proverbs 2
by John Stanko
Copyright ©2022 John Stanko

ISBN 978-1-63360-196-3

For Worldwide Distribution
Printed in the U.S.A.

Urban Press
P.O. Box 8881
Pittsburgh, PA 15221-0881
412.646.2780
www.urbanpress.us

INTRODUCTION

The worldwide pandemic began in March of 2020. At first we thought it would end in a few weeks, then in a few months, then a few more months, but certainly we thought it would be over a year later. Unfortunately, it was not and as I write, we are still seeing it quite active in various parts of the world, with an uncertain future ahead as to its course and severity.

Who could ever forget those days of social distancing, isolation, quarantine, mask wearing, shifting regulations, arguments over the effectiveness of various treatments and preventions, and uncertainty concerning when life would resume with some semblance of normalcy — or even if it ever would? My own posture during the pandemic was that we were in it for the long haul, and I prepared mentally for a long break from what I had been doing, especially traveling.

Fortunately for me, I had my computer and the Internet, which is all I needed to get by. I stationed myself at my desk at 6 a.m. and sometimes I would still be there at 10:00 p.m. I wrote and published seven books in 2021 and finished many more for others through my publishing company. One of those books was *Pandemic Proverbs: Wisdom for Troubled Times*, which was a compilation of my short sayings I published online almost daily throughout the turbulent days of the pandemic.

For me, the pandemic was a chance to prove what I had been writing and teaching about — social media was and is a gift from God, something He wanted His people and His church to utilize. I have maintained that it is possible to build and maintain relationships online through a regular presence that does more than complain about politicians, celebrate sports victories, or publish the latest family pictures. I believed and set out to prove that regular posts and entries with content that others needed and valued establishes a bond between writer or speaker and reader that enhances meaningful relationships.

That conclusion flies in the face of common sense that would say relationships need to be face-to-face to be real. I am 72 years old as I write and my generation is suspect of social media at best and loathes it at worst. We have grudgingly given in to its presence but we see it as an encroachment upon our privacy, dismissing it as anything but a useful means of communication, except in emergencies.

Oh, but the technology is a blessing if it helps us connect with our grandchildren or use our phones hands free in our cars or helps us pay a bill that is close to being overdue. My point is we curse technology until it serves our purposes to remain connected to those who are important to us through the very technology and social media we resent. However, let me descend from my soapbox and tell you a bit more about this second volume of *Pandemic Proverbs* that you hold in your hand.

When I was a young Christian in the '80s, I did some work for a Christian magazine that had a worldwide circulation of 100,000. Every month, the magazine would focus on one theme — finances, family, prayer, missions — and invariably we would receive letters saying, "How did you know? That magazine theme spoke to the very issues God was emphasizing in our lives at that time. Thank you!"

When you stop to think of it, that magazine was a form of technology and was the precursor to what we have today via social media. I learned that God could use something that was "mass produced" and make it something personal for the readers. My thinking was, *If God did that with a magazine, why couldn't He do the same with social media?* Of course, my answer to the question was, *He can,* which is why I am so radically committed to an all-day, every-day presence online.

Since I am also an author and publisher, then it made sense to compile and publish what I spent so much time doing online — thus the two volumes of *Pandemic Proverbs.* As in the volume one, you will find some material that is repeated throughout the book. Repetition is never a bad thing and I use the book of Proverbs as proof, for it repeats sayings throughout its 31 chapters. I guess God wanted to make sure we got the message, and thus, I use the same technique.

Also, there are prayers scattered throughout this volume, and they are in italics. Since I published most of my prayers on Mondays, you may see that I used then to pray for the coming week. I didn't change that when I decided to include them in his volume. Remember also that a proverb doesn't have to represent all the truth about a matter, but rather presents a truth for thought and reflection. It's interesting to me that I will post a 15-word proverb online, only to have people respond with a 250-word entry picking apart my short little proverb. Don't try to make these entries any more than they are intended to be; just accept them as a thought teaser. If you disagree, just move on. Who knows, maybe the idea in that entry will make more sense later.

I confess that I have enjoyed my online work in presenting these thoughts to a worldwide audience, and I take it seriously as I sit many mornings and ask, *Well, God, what can I write today?* There were times when I almost didn't publish something, only to think, *If this post helps one person, it's worth it. Let's put it out there.* More often than not, the post did help someone, which only reinforced my premise that social media is God's gift — if we use it properly.

John Stanko
Pittsburgh, Pennsylvania, USA
May 2022

Lord, open my eyes to all my opportunities this week to serve You and others.

Lord, let's partner this week to touch lives. I will launch the words; You pick them up and transport them in the power of the Spirit.

If your foot is nailed to the floor and you're going around in circles, the answer isn't to go faster; it's to get free.

Paul wrote in Colossians 1:13 that God has transferred our citizenship from the kingdom of darkness to the kingdom of His beloved Son.

You don't need great faith. Jesus said mustard-seed-sized faith is enough to do great things.

I'm happy to play for either a full house or a private performance.

Don't focus on your limitations; focus on the unlimited power of the same Spirit that raised Christ from the dead living in you.

The enemy of your soul is a terrorist and uses fear to keep you from stepping up and out into your purpose and creativity.

What you see is so clear, you assume others must be blind if they don't see it, but they're not. It's unique to you, which is why you must speak, act, write, teach — to share the insight that comes from your purpose.

Very often the testimony you don't want to give is the testimony you need to give.

The joy of the Lord is your strength; that's the reason you must do what gives you joy as often as possible.

What could you accomplish today if you weren't afraid: afraid it won't be good enough, afraid you don't have enough time, afraid you're out of God's will, afraid of rejection or ridicule?

Paul wrote Timothy that out of all his persecutions and troubles, the Lord delivered him. He'll do the same for you.

The church isn't a spiritual country club or a social organization.

Acts 14:22 — "We must go through *many* hardships to enter the kingdom of God."

This is no time to go into hibernation; this is a time to gear up for growth and productivity.

If your present path is difficult, it is *not* an indication you missed the Lord. It may be a confirmation you heard Him.

Your life purpose is the only thing that's too good to be true — but it's true. You get to do what you love as often as possible.

Build bridges, not forts. Ask questions, don't preach. Choose service, not power.

You're disturbed because you are disturb-able. Perhaps your problem isn't external; it's internal.

God, I'm not concerned so much with whether people like me or not; just don't let them ignore me and what You've given me to say and do.

You have everything you need for today; when you get to tomorrow, what you need will be there as well.

God, I don't want an ordinary week; I want an extraordinary one in You.

Whining is the opposite of praise; grumbling is the opposite of thanksgiving.

Today would be a good day to do an inventory of all God's blessings in your life, past and present.

Without faith, it's impossible to please God. That means with faith it's possible to please God. Choose to please God today.

There's no baby or adolescent Holy Spirit. If a youth has faith, it's the same as an adult's faith. Trust God no matter how young or old you are.

Faith motivates you to expand your world; fear causes you to shrink its size so you can control your world.

Faith never requires you to ignore the facts; it simply requires that the facts not have the final say as to what you will do.

The crazy-makers in your life are sapping your strength and joy; time to establish some boundaries.

The devil is a master strategist; he has successfully divided the Church, and an army that divides its troops in battle is in trouble.

If all your advisors are just like you, then they aren't advisors, they are your bodyguards, protecting you from change.

You will eventually act out what you think about, so if you aren't pleased with your life, the change starts between your ears.

"Oh, I can't take all the junk on social media!" Why are you reading junk? Produce quality stuff to counteract the junk.

You don't need someone to console you; you need someone to punch you in your spiritual gut and take your breath away.

"I'll do this or that once the weather is cooler, or when the kids go back to school, or after the election, or after the holidays." All those are excuses (lies even) and if truth be told, you won't unless you change the way you think.

You haven't given enough grace to others until someone accuses you of giving too much.

"Above all else, *guard your heart*, for everything you do flows from it" (Proverbs 4:23, emphasis added). Where is your heart these days?

I want to write things that will bring a smile, not pain; peace, not anger; kindness, not accusation.

Power unless tempered by service to others has the tendency to intoxicate our judgment. We eventually believe we deserved or earned our leadership position.

Anyone can learn how to behave for two hours on Sunday, but it's the other 166 hours every week that are the true test of the depth and reality of one's walk with the Lord.

The Church is limping, dying in some cases, while our passions and interests lie in other areas.

God's purpose isn't for us to sing in one accord but to act in one accord. The latter is much harder to achieve.

Breaking a promise you made to yourself is as serious an ethical breach as when you break a promise to others.

What difference will God's presence in your life make today? Or will it be business as usual?

Time to emerge from your cave of anonymity into the sunlight of creativity.

One of the key elements in winning is not quitting. Don't give up.

An idol isn't something you worship *instead* of God but that you worship *along with* God.

There's unique music in you. It's time to sing your song, not hum the tune of others.

You learn to make good decisions through the experience of having made bad ones — and heeding their lessons.

Paul was in prison and everyone was against him. It was then that the Lord stood by his side, but also told him he was going to encounter more of the same. God won't apologize for the cross He has assigned you to carry.

"Excuse me, Lord, but I have much to say and many needs, so please don't interrupt my prayer." Listen and don't talk so much.

God can use an organization to provide for you, but He doesn't need one. He can use a fish, a raven, or a widow, or take the little you have and never let it run out.

There's no more courageous act than being the person God made you to be.

You want to be normal so others will accept or like you, but normal for you lies in your uniqueness, not your conformity.

Where did some get the idea that taking care of God's money means one must be stingy or cheap? God loves a cheerful, generous giver.

"The secret of change is to focus all your energy, not on fighting the old, but on building the new."
— Socrates

For many years, I ignored what God wanted me to do so I could fit in and be a good team player. No more. "Put me in, Coach."

Lord, I rest in You this week, but when You show me the need or opportunity, I'm on it!

You are waiting on the Lord, but could it be that He is waiting on you too?

Zeal for His house and not the House (or Senate) must consume us.

Do you have too much clutter in your life? When in doubt, throw it out. "I may need this" thinking is bogging you down with unneeded stuff.

Are you fatigued and don't know why? Could it be that boredom is causing you to work hard just to get through the day? There's a better way.

When you think you're the most important part of the team, you cease to be the most important part of the team.

If you don't get control of your thought life, you won't rest even when you rest. Time to think new thoughts.

Today Jesus would say, "Out of a person's heart, their social media posts flow." Where's your heart these days?

"Christ in you, the hope of glory" means God lives in you and has access to you — but you also have access to Him.

God, my insight from last week isn't enough for this week. I need more, Lord — more of You, Your Word, Your wisdom.

You need Jesus but He needs you, and is enlisting you in the great work of proclaiming and establishing His Kingdom.

Stop denying the essence of who you are — that is *not* your cross to bear. Your cross isn't doing what you hate; it's doing what you love but perhaps in a place or with people you're not fond of.

Your job is to make a difference, not to make a ruckus.

We don't realize how far Adam and Eve "fell" until we start the journey back to wholeness and obedience. It's a long road home.

There's always someone smarter or more gifted than you, so stop comparing yourself to others and just be the best you that you can be.

You are the instrument the Lord plays to attract, inspire, entertain, instruct, or comfort others. Make sure you stay in tune.

The preacher/teacher should ask with each message, "What do I want this message to produce in the hearer? What has it produced in me?"

You can love money even though you don't have any.

Hannah proves God hears the cries of your heart you can't even articulate.

The Temple proves God can use a building, but He won't hesitate to tear it down when it becomes an idol.

The rich young ruler proves God isn't after your money; He's after *you*.

Solomon proves you can have a lot of wisdom yet not apply it to your own life.

God doesn't want more of you; He wants *all* of you — for your own good.

Paul proves you can do your best writing in less than ideal surroundings (like jail or quarantine).

Esther proves your past does not dictate your future.

Don't brag that you've had multiple confirmations of a word from the Lord while you still haven't done much with it. That's not spirituality; it's disobedience.

You have a chance to impact the direction and tone of your conversations today in a way that will bring peace.

To be a good writer, preacher, teacher, poet, or business person, you must be willing to be bad at it for a while.

"You need to persevere so that when you have done the will of God, you will receive what he has promised" (Hebrews 10:36).

Don't give up.

The devil isn't your biggest problem just yet; *you* are your biggest problem. Get out of your own way and be fruitful.

"No weapon formed" actually means *a lot* of weapons will be formed and used against you. It's just that none of them will succeed.

Abraham was taking his only son to sacrifice but told his servants, "*We will* be back." Now *that's* faith.

If God wants you to start an online cooking show, teaching show, kids show, arts and crafts show, or any other show, *do it.*

To achieve your purpose, you may have to abandon your current audience and go find a new one.

God, I'm ready to act or not, go or not, speak or not, write or not. Direct me this week into Your daily will.

To succeed in your purpose, you have to be willing to go through hell to achieve heavenly results.

God, it's not about me this week; it's about You and Your people. My time is Yours — and theirs.

"Unless a kernel of wheat falls to the ground and dies, it remains only a single seed. But if it dies, it produces many seeds" (John 12:24). Succeeding in your purpose will require you to die to self to the extent you never thought possible.

Jesus said His followers would do greater things than He did. What are your greater things?

While it's nice if people *like* what you post or do, it's not really an indication of how many people *see* what you do. Stop looking at the numbers.

Develop your gift, God will use you. Neglect your gift, people will use you.

Faith is like a muscle; the more you use it, the stronger it gets. Are you in need of some exercise?

God, I trust You for time this week to do what's most important to You, not me. Guide my priorities.

They accused Jesus, the sinless Son of God, of being in league with the devil, but He turned their insult into a teaching opportunity. No need to take things personally.

Some people have so many "pet" peeves they could open a zoo. Time to chill out and lighten up.

Lord, I've laid out my week. Now interrupt and adjust where necessary.

Success isn't something you wait for; it's something you prepare for.

David was faithful in the cave and on the run, so God gave him a throne. God knows how to prepare and promote.

Smaller isn't better, bigger isn't more spiritual. It's obedience, not results, that matters most.

Your soul is too big to be fed by one person on one day of the week. This is why the early church met *daily*.

It used to be leaders were made in the church and went out to the world; now they are made in the world and come to the church. There's a big difference between the two based on their worldview of problems and their solutions.

Why would God want you to do His will but then make it hard to discover what it is? Could your fear be the hang up?

"The world's watching us." I'm not sure they are. How can they "see" us unless they come to where we are?

Jesus often said for "it" to be done according to one's faith. What is the "it" for which you have faith to see or do?

Your job is not to be a judge or evaluator of ministry, but a producer of ministry.

God isn't looking for balanced people; He's looking for those who know when and how to give their all as they go through an open door.

Wait on the Lord,
but when He speaks,
it's time to move!

Jesus is looking for agents
who He can live in and work
through to achieve greater
things. It's no longer you who
live, but Christ who lives in you.

You'll only know how far you
can go when you're willing to
risk going too far.

Don't wait for God to change
things in you He has no
intention of changing. God can
use you as you are while He
transforms you into a better
version of who you are.

A purpose pastor's job is to help
people know their gifts and
purpose and then help them
overcome the fear that comes
with expressing them.

Zechariah 4:10 – "Who dares
despise the day of small things?"

Because you can't do a lot,
you still shouldn't hesitate
to do a little.

Seasons of discipline are like braces on your teeth. God is exerting gentle but consistent pressure to bring about permanent change.

Your greater test may be how you handle success rather than failure.

Our pain and frustrations are simply reminders that we are pilgrims passing through to the Promised Land. The best is yet to come!

If you think you can, you probably will; if you think you can't, you won't even try.

Saying what you will do "one day" is often a sedative that lulls you to sleep during which you can substitute dreams for reality.

"Pray, ask for wisdom, listen, have faith, and act" is the formula to follow if you need to hear from the Lord.

You're one phone call,
one meeting, one email away
from a breakthrough.
Stay hopeful and vigilant.

*God, the good can be
the enemy of the best.
I want the best this week.*

God won't tolerate in you what
He seems to overlook in others.
Don't whine — it's part of your
training for reigning.

Jesus came not to look good,
but to do good, which is why He
looked bad to those who only
wanted to look good.

*It's no more work to write for
many than a few, so expand my
audience this week, Lord. I want
to touch many lives!*

Zany prophetic end-time
predictions should not be the
essence of a prophetic ministry.
Prophets are to equip the saints
for their ministry work,
not entertain.

"I surrender all"
cannot be just a song;
it has to be a way of life.

Biblical preaching is not a
talk about the Word;
it *explains* the Word with
attention to application.

It's remarkable how much
light the Bible sheds on its
commentaries. Stop reading
about the Word; read the Word.

Your job isn't to shrink your
world to a controllable size but
to expand it so you can touch
and serve as many as possible.

Fear of others will cause you to
play smaller than you are. Time
to speak up, step up, and make
up for lost time.

Lord, I put aside distractions
this week so I can keep
the main things the main thing.

God, help me manage my time
and the opportunities that
surround me this week.

If you do what you do only
for money, no matter how
noble it is, you're nothing
but a hired gun going to
the highest bidder.

Christianity and power
are incompatible.
We are to influence others,
not control them.

You have one life purpose,
but it can be expressed in
many ways through your
unique gifts and creativity.

The Christmas story
reveals God's grand plan
for dealing with sin.

If Judas didn't kiss Jesus,
the soldiers would not have
known who to arrest.
Leaders should seek to blend in,
not stand out.

Some of us want overnight delivery but only have regular mail faith.

We are called to change, not rearrange.

God can use an organization or company to pay you, but He doesn't need one to do so.

God seldom gives you the resources you need until you trust Him by creating the need for the resources. You act, then God.

In some games, the clock may say 0:00 but you can still win the game. It's not over until God says it's over. Don't give up.

Food, clothing, shelter, health, provision, purpose, His presence — God has done His part; now I must do mine, and you yours.

If you're ignorant and
God anoints you,
don't think the anointing
will overcome your ignorance.

Do the work.

The Christmas story shows that
sometimes God bypasses the
religious establishment and goes
right to the people.

Genesis Joseph proves that
if you make someone else's
dream come true, there's
something in it for you, too.

What I get I will give, what I hear
I will say, what I think of I will do
every day this week.

The psalms prove you can say
anything to God and it may not
change your circumstances —
but it will change you.

*God, I don't want You to
fill my cup to overflowing;
I want a bigger cup.*

If you already know
what you want to start doing
on January 2, why not start
today and get a head start?

Bezalel's creativity wasn't a
hobby; it was his mandate
from the Lord. What about
yours? Are you using it
as God intended?

Are you discouraged?
Then today find someone to
encourage because you of all
people know how it feels.

Spiritual gluttony is
consistently taking in more
spiritual sustenance than you
expend in your own ministry.

Don't be a fat saint.

Faith isn't an event,
it's a lifestyle;
not a last resort,
but a first response.

Zachariah 4:10 —
"Do not despise these
small beginnings . . ."
You have to start someplace.
Why not start today where you
are with what you have?

If no one or no group
helps you with your purpose,
then get started and
God will be your Helper.

*Lord, empower me
to empower others.*

God didn't apologize to Mary;
He sent her a messenger to
tell her how blessed and favored
she was even though her life
from that time forward
would be difficult.

Be careful that your obsession
with not getting ahead of the
Lord doesn't cause you to fall
behind His pace for your life.

*Lord, I don't want to be
a giver only during Christmas
week; help me make it
a year-round lifestyle*

Church is a few hours of
the 168 hours in a week.
It's easy to learn what to do
in those church hours,
but it's the rest of your time
that makes the difference in
your walk with the Lord.

"This one thing I do, not these many things I dabble with"
— Dwight Moody.

If your creativity is a gift, then it can't be a hobby; it must take center stage in your life's performance.

Stop being content with getting wet and treading water; it's time to swim in the deep end.

Yes, Lord, I want more money to do more good works.

An eagle acting like a chicken would be humorous and strange. The same is true for you when you try to be less than who God made you to be.

As the song says, "More love, more power, more of You in my life."

Lord, I'm not content to watch You work. I want to be working along with You as long as I have strength.

God, my job isn't to judge and critique others but to encourage and equip them.

I don't care what you're going to do this year, I want to know what you're going to do *today* that contributes to what you're going to do this year.

God is *not* obligated to share His future plans with those who have a desire to predict the future for others on His behalf.

God, I need to stop doing some things, even though I enjoy them, to do other new things. Time to release and move on.

I've already lived through several failed predictions that the Lord was returning in my lifetime. If Jesus didn't know when He was coming back, I doubt if any modern prophet knows either.

The Word tells me *not* to despise prophecy but also to *judge* it, not accept it at face value.

"You did not choose me, but I chose you and appointed you so that you might go and bear fruit — fruit that will last — and so that whatever you ask in my name the Father will give you" (John 15:16). Where's your fruit?

If prophets deliver the word of the Lord, then aren't pastors and preachers who stand in the pulpit just as prophetic as future tellers?

I have an urgency to do what I do and say what I say like never before. All my goals are *now* goals, not future goals.

A personal prophecy is like an old picture negative; it must be developed or else it's useless.

My chosen epitaph: "Here lies a courageous man of purpose." For that to be true, it's what I need to be today and every day.

My legacy won't be how many people I exposed who were wrong, but how many I helped to be right (with Him).

God, show me new ways to do old things in this season.

God, open my eyes to what You're doing and the changes You're bringing.

"No one from the east or the west or from the desert can exalt themselves. It is God who judges: He brings one down, he exalts another" (Psalm 75:6-7). God has His own plans, and He isn't obligated to share or explain them to anyone.

I complained once, "I'm not selling many books." The Lord responded, "Who said you have to sell them?"

The world expects two things from the Church: love and care for the poor. If every church would focus on those practices, we would radically change the way we think about and conduct the business of church.

Just because the world's gone crazy doesn't mean you need to follow its lead or example.

Stop waiting for the church to do *your* job or to provide a platform for *you* to fulfill *your* purpose.

I've taught for many years that changing the way we do church starts with *you* finding and fulfilling your purpose.

It isn't time to storm the walls of government; it's time to storm the gates of hell.

If your church doesn't feed the poor, then *you* do it. Don't excuse your inactivity because of what others aren't doing.

This isn't a day to mourn the past but to take steps to get better at what you're gifted to do and find new ways to do it.

Prayer of St. Augustine: "Increase my desire for You, God, that I might be able to receive what You are preparing to give me."

God wants to lead you to a land flowing with milk and honey and get you out of the desert where you only get bread and water.

Your choice.

If God could use Samson, He can use anyone — including you. Your past failures don't determine your future effectiveness, *unless* you allow them to do so.

God has invested much in you, but He expects a return on His investment.

God doesn't owe you a full explanation before you take your first step; He will reveal Himself *as* you go, not *before* you go.

God is love, so any work you do *not* motivated by love can't be from God.

God has provided for His people through a raven, a ram, a fish, manna, and quail; there is no limit to how God can provide for you. Do God's will (your job) and let Him provide as He chooses (His job).

Lord, by Your grace I'll keep the main thing the main thing this week, and that's fulfilling the purpose You assigned me.

I'm seldom scandalized or surprised by the sins or behavior of others because I have had to face the depths of my own depravity along with the heights of God's grace.

The insight and wisdom I had last week aren't enough for this week. I need more, Lord, much more.

I'm fascinated to see some people who object to being "lumped together" as a group doing the same thing to those they dislike.

God, I must be a good steward of the energy You give me and not dissipate it on matters not relevant to You or Your kingdom.

"Human anger (outrage, indignation, ire, rage, wrath) does not produce the righteousness that God desires" (James 1:20).

God may have you be a part of the solution to a problem you didn't cause. If you refuse, you'll become part of the problem.

"What if what I'm thinking isn't of the Lord?" Better question: "What if it is?"

If you're walking a new road, look for a guide who has walked down that same road, not someone who has only heard about it.

Ask yourself "What did I do as a child that I no longer do because I 'grew up'? Does that have anything to do with my purpose?"

I owe allegiance to the Kingdom above country, race, party, ethnicity, church, culture, tradition, or family.

The Kingdom isn't a democracy; we don't get a vote, only a voice.

While China terrorizes the world, God terrorizes China as the church continues to grow, despite persecution.

It's not about what church you're in, it's all about what kingdom you're in.

If all that is happening is the "end" and is playing out as we have been told it would, then the saints should be the happiest people earth.

The devil is the prince of the power of the air (see Ephesians 2:2) and understands all too well how to use media and rumors to disrupt and disturb.

A new you among old friends isn't always recognized or appreciated. Time for some new friends?

Procrastination isn't the same thing as waiting on the Lord. The first is rooted in fear, the second in faith.

When you mess up, it's not time to run *from* God but time to run *to* God.

God doesn't want you to maintain your world, He wants you to expand your world. Do you have a maintenance or expansion mindset?

An idol in your life doesn't mean you've turned from God; you just learn to worship the idol along with God.

Give yourself permission to be who God made you to be. No need to apologize to anyone.

Time always proves God knew what He was doing when in the short run you weren't so sure.

How much does God love diversity? Seven billion people on the planet and *everyone* has a unique set of fingerprints.

When you denigrate who you are, don't be offended when others do the same.

How are your annual goals and resolutions coming along?

Unforgiveness is bitter but drink it long enough and you can get used to the flavor.

Go where you're celebrated, not tolerated.

Our desire to know the future has caused us to seek wisdom from sources, even in the church, that are best left alone.

God doesn't explain Himself to us; we wouldn't understand it anyway.

God can make you a household name or put your face on a billboard and doesn't need your permission — but He needs your cooperation.

Any principle that always "works" to get God to respond or do what you want has become your god.

Pretending to be small when God has made you big dishonors His will for your life. Release your gift and work to make it all it can be.

God never apologizes for what you go through, but promises to always go through it with you.

Success is doing what you love as often as possible; money is a byproduct of that, not the main objective.

Overwhelmed? Sorrowful? Perplexed? Oppressed? Busy? Confused? "My grace is sufficient for Thee" — 2 Corinthians 12:9.

The Bible doesn't describe Paul's thorn in the flesh; you don't need to know what his was, you only need to know what *yours* is.

"I have been crucified with Christ and I no longer live, but Christ lives in me. The life I now live in the body, I live by faith in the Son of God, who loved me and gave himself for me" — Galatians 2:20.

Maybe the prophet didn't mean this is your year of breakthrough but rather brokenness?

What you are suffering and encountering are part of God's discipline, and evidence of His love. Don't despair.

You can trust the joy of the Lord because it doesn't emanate from your emotions; it's the fruit of the Spirit's presence in your life.

Matthew 5:8 — "Blessed are the pure in heart, for they will see God." Having trouble seeing God?' Then check the purity of your own heart.

We're so concerned about going too far that we often don't go far enough, thus never exploring the farthest boundaries of our purpose and creativity.

Lord, use what I do in word or deed this week to encourage, inspire, and edify others.

The pandemic has reminded us that the end is *always* near for every one of us as well as for the things we take for granted.

God, make me a better writer to better communicate the better things You want us to know and see.

God isn't a passive God and therefore isn't looking for a passive people. He's actively doing good and expects us to do the same.

We must address the
ills of society without being
consumed by those ills —
or our anger over them.

The four lepers asked, "Why sit
we here until we die?" That's
a good question for you today.
Why are you sitting in the same
place but expecting some kind
of breakthrough or victory?
Time to move out and up.

Leave your current support
group that helps you go
nowhere and establish a new
one that will help you
go somewhere.

Time to re-read Revelation, not
to focus on the antichrist or the
beast, but rather to see how
exalted and victorious
the Christ of God is.

What could you do today if
you weren't afraid of starting?
of failing? of making a mistake?
of looking foolish?

You talk and sing big,
but then do you
work and play small?

Psalm 146:3 — "Do not put your
trust in princes,
in human beings,
who cannot save."

First you were too young, now
you say you're too old. Faith
doesn't have an expiration date
that comes with it.

The message of Revelation is
this: *Many* rivals to the Lamb
who sits on the throne will
emerge, some human, others
in the form of philosophies,
but they will *all* fail to dethrone
Him — but will certainly try.

If you're willing to do
more than you're paid to do,
eventually you'll be paid for
more than you do.

A message of Revelation:
Any people or nation that
doesn't serve the Lamb is
destined to become a beast.

Don't form a belief and then
look for a Bible verse to prove
it; read the Bible and form your
belief around what you read.

Birds don't sing because they have an audience or are paid to sing; they sing because they are birds. What were you created to do? *Do it!*

Treat those who don't think, believe, or vote like you as a mission field, not as a battlefield.

No one can tell you what should or should not be in your heart, what you should or should not do. That role is reserved for God.

"Love your neighbor as yourself" *except* for those who don't vote like you?

You may know your purpose, but now God wants to show you where to express it. It may not be close to home or with those who look like you.

Stop acting like the "other side" of how you voted has *nothing* to teach you.

When we demonize those who don't think or vote like us, we are missing the fact that there are *real* demons oppressing our cities, youth, and churches. Time to fight our true enemies.

Someone in the worst church with bad singing and mediocre preaching is *still* in a better place than going to hell; church needs to get people to live right, not vote right.

God, help me write, create, and shape things and experiences that will take people's breath away and cause them to say "praise the Lord."

Heaven doesn't stand at attention or kneel when *The Star Spangled Banner* is played.

Be careful when a slogan summarizes who you are; there's more to you and certainly more to your faith than that.

Paul wrote "desire earnestly to prophesy" in 1 Corinthians 14:39; we need a better understanding of New Testament prophets.

We tend to repent for things we have done but seldom for the good things we neglected to do.

If God can do exceedingly abundantly beyond all we can ask or think, then how can we get ahead of Him? How can we do too much good? How can we express our gifts to serve others too often?

When you spy out God's Promised Land for you, what do you see? Giants or possibilities? Fear or faith? Your inadequacy or God's greatness?

Church is not the destination, but rather a filling station on the way to your ultimate purpose destination.

John 1:14 – "We saw his glory, such glory as of the one and only Son of the Father, full of grace and truth." God, help us to embody those two words that seem to contradict one another: grace and truth.

The truth will *not* set you free unless you want it to do so. Until then, a lie will keep you in bondage.

Lord, this week my path will be strewn with opportunities; give me eyes to see them.

Colossians 1:10 – "So that you may live a life worthy of the Lord and please him in every way: bearing fruit in every good work, growing in the knowledge of God."

God, help me examine my thoughts this week; show me where I'm limiting You or what You want me to do or be.

God, help me to live a life worthy of You by bearing fruit and growing in Your knowledge.

Lord, I need more: more love, more insight, more heart, more wisdom this week.

Boredom is God's herald announcing there's something wrong and it's time to move on.

Your daily routine is not sacred, so don't be upset when the Sacred interrupts it.

What if God doesn't want to take something away to lighten your life, but instead wants to give you more so He can help you carry your burden?

What if God doesn't want to change what you think needs changed, but instead wants to develop what you don't want to develop?

Psalm 139:23-24 — "Search me, God, and know my heart; test me and know my anxious thoughts. See if there is any offensive way in me, and lead me in the way everlasting." Pray that prayer today and then actively seek to change who you are and what you do.

What if God desires you to step out, not step back?

What if you are at peace because you have hardened your heart and stiffened your neck?

Jesus said His yoke is easy and His burden light. If you're carrying something heavy and it's weighing you down, it's not His yoke.

God, help me say more with less words. Help me do more with less time. Help me reach more with less effort.

I may not say it all the time, but we need to "change the way we do church" to reach more people through new strategies.

Faith isn't a pill you swallow when you're in need, but rather the spiritual vitamins you take every day.

Your *test* leads to a *testi*mony through which you at*test* to the goodness and faithfulness of God.

Your creativity isn't a hobby; it's to be expressed as often as possible. When you do that, you honor the One who gave it to you.

David learned more about leadership from Saul than anyone else; he learned how *not* to lead. God will put you in a bad situation to learn; make sure you don't replicate what you experienced when you eventually lead.

Lamentations 3:22-23 — "The steadfast love of the Lord never ceases; his mercies never come to an end; they are new every morning; great is your faithfulness."

Galatians 6:7 — "Do not be deceived: God cannot be mocked. A man reaps what he sows." Your lack today is because you underestimated how much you would have to sow yesterday to get what you need tomorrow.

No one is ever a complete failure, for they may serve as a horrible example from whom others may learn.

Job 1:21 — "Naked I came from my mother's womb, and naked I shall return there. The Lord gave and the Lord has taken away. Blessed be the name of the Lord."

You can't give what you don't have. That's why you build yourself up first and then look to build others.

Your decision not to do something is actually a decision to do something, which is nothing.

Faith is like riding a roller coaster. You're scared during the ride but can't wait to do it again when it's over.

Don't give so God will bless you, but when you give, God will bless you.

Worry isn't just a bad habit, it's a sin habit. You learned to worry, so you can unlearn it too. "Be anxious for *nothing*."

You can't want something for someone more than they want it for themselves. Time to let it and them go free of your expectations.

Encouragement is
oxygen for the soul;
don't let someone close to you
suffer from spiritual asphyxiation.

There are crazy-makers addicted
to drama who want you to play
a supporting role in their movie;
don't go there even —
if they're family.

It's good to wait on the Lord,
just make sure He's not
waiting on you.

Psalm 95:7b — "Today, if only
you would hear his voice."
That is the great need of any
saint. *Do you hear His voice?*

Write two pages per day
for 45 days and voila!
You will have your manuscript.

The message of the prophets
(and the Church) should be
to exalt Jesus, focusing on His
majesty and Lordship —
not current events.

Don't confuse your job
with your purpose.
Your job gives you money, your
purpose gives you joy.
To combine them both is a gift.

Ananias prayed for Saul
and the scales fell from Saul's
eyes so he could see his purpose.
Pray today that your eyes will
be opened to see what
God has for you to do.

In Acts 9, Dorcas proves a
woman with a heart for the
poor and a sewing machine can
capture the attention of heaven.

Your prophetic ministry isn't
based on telling the future but
interpreting the past as to what
Christ has done and how your
listeners can apply what He did
in their daily lives.

Barnabas' apostolic calling came
from his ability to encourage
others. Stop looking for
something great to do;
just find something simple
to do and do it greatly.

Our zany interpretations of the
end times have produced fear
and anxiety in our hearts instead
of an eager anticipation, coupled
with a pursuit of holiness,
that the Lord is coming soon.

God's sending revival but it's not what you think. It's not to get more people *into* the church but to get them *out* of the church and *into* their purpose. It's a purpose revival.

1 John 5:2 — "This is how we know that we love the children of God: by loving God and carrying out his commands."

God lives in you, but it's your job to make Him feel at home.

Isaiah 6:1 — "In the year that King Uzziah died, I saw the Lord, high and exalted, seated on a throne." There's a throne in heaven that is *never* empty even when the ones on earth are (or are poorly filled).

The *same* Spirit that raised Christ from the dead dwells in you. Is resurrection power evident in what you do and who you are?

The disciples were to wait for power from on high in the person of the Holy Spirit. Do you have the Spirit? Do you have the *power* of the Spirit? What are you em*power*ed to do?

You proclaim the Kingdom by telling His story and explaining how your story fits into His story.

Lord, this week help me press on and press through the obstacles to bearing fruit and serving You and others.

Luke 6:26 — "Woe to you when everyone speaks well of you." Following God's Kingdom rule should cause someone to be upset with you.

God, I need to be better at what I do this week than last. I need more grace, more strength, more faith.

You are a witness, which means you give your life to a cause; that's why people must see you and how you live out the Kingdom.

John 2:23-24 — "Many believed in His name . . . but Jesus did not commit Himself to them." Can Jesus commit Himself to you?

Jesus can't commit all of Himself to you until you commit all of yourself to Him.

My definition of excellence is doing all you do from a right heart and in a manner worthy of God. That doesn't require perfection.

Isaiah 45:22 – "Look to Me, and be saved, all you ends of the earth! For I am God, and there is no other." There's *no* other name under heaven by which people can be saved.

If you take in more spiritual calories then you expend, you'll get spiritually chubby. You then lose weight by exercising your faith.

Your lack of progress in writing is because you want to be writer *and* editor. Just write and edit when you're done, *not* before.

I want to be a master at what I do because the best make it simple for others to do as well. *Lord, make me good at what I do.*

Editing your creative work before it's done is like eating raw meat; cook it first, *then* season it, reheat it, and serve it as is.

Faith shows you the future so clearly that you can walk in it today before others see it.

Failure is like an expensive steak dinner. You paid a high price for it, so make sure you get the most out of it.

A goal with a plan is your spiritual GPS that tells you how to get from where you are to where you want or need to go.

It's a trap to think that all you have to do is believe right without having to live the right you believe. You may fool some people, but you won't fool God.

What you want people to say at your funeral is an indication of what you need to be doing today and every day. What do you want your legacy to be?

Even the stock market is innovating how it functions, but much of the church languishes for lack of creativity.

If you worship at the altar of your privacy, Jesus can still invite a group of people to watch you do it.

Deuteronomy 29:29 — "The secret things belong to the Lord our God, but those things which are revealed belong to us and to our children forever, that we may do all the words of this law."

Stop whining; start winning.

Leadership isn't learning how to wield power; it's learning how to give it away to empower others.

Those who have a small version of God think small thoughts.

Paul prayed "that you may be filled with all the fullness of God" (Ephesians 3:19). Are you? What proof do you have?

God, make me better at what I do; allow me to touch more with any insight You choose to give me.

Ephesians 3:20 – "Now to Him who is able to do exceedingly abundantly above all that we ask or think, according to the power that works in us." What do you have power to do?

Romans 1:14 – "I am a debtor both to Greeks and to barbarians, both to wise and to unwise." *Yes, Lord, I too owe You and Your people.*

Black leader Booker T. Washington, founder of Tuskegee, was asked if he took vacations: "And stop doing what I love to do nothing?" That's the power of purpose. Until you find it, you won't know what he was talking about.

My words and presence are inadequate, Lord, to get my job done. Expand my heart and mind to love more, do more, see more.

God, I don't want to play on the playground; I want to swim in the ocean, fly in the sky, climb on Your mountain.

God, may I never be content with where I am or what I have in You. May my motto always be one simple word: more.

God, I heard You call me to Africa. Yet doors are closed and time is short. Make a way, Lord, make a way.

God, wrong is right, shame is honorable, ugliness the preferred dress. Never before has the beauty of holiness been more needed.

God, Your church, Your church. Shake us from our slumber, deliver us from our folly, revive us in our purpose.

Time to get rid of the clutter — on your desk, around your house, in your mind. Don't waste time going through your stuff to get to your stuff.

God may not deliver you from trouble but He will preserve you in the midst of it.

You're one call, email, or chance meeting away from your breakthrough. Stay ready and hopeful.

Colossians 3:3 – "Your life is now hidden with Christ in God." For something to get to you, it must first get His permission.

One minute Joseph was in jail, the next minute he was standing before Pharaoh, and the next he was the vice president. It took him 13 years to get his breakthrough but he was *ready*. Be prepared; stay hopeful.

Proverbs 16:3 (AMPC) – "He will cause your thoughts to be agreeable to his will and so shall your plans be established and succeed." You are thinking the thoughts of God.

Wishing something so doesn't make something so. It takes preparation, diligence, and faith in God — along with the work He has done in you.

If you think you can't, you won't.
If you think you may, you might.
If you think you will, you do.

What could you do
if you were not afraid of
going too far or failing?

Stop whining,
start writing.

Philippians 4:13 – "I can do all things through Christ who strengthens me." Comforting saying, but what are the *all things* you are doing?

God doesn't owe you an audience or a market; you have to earn those for yourself.

You won't know how far you can go until you risk going too far.

You do good deeds
not to earn God's favor
but because you have it.

Don't tell others where to
go or what to do; take them
there through your example,
leadership, and companionship.

The best way to
meet your needs
is by meeting
the needs of others.

If the King is making all things
new, what's *new* in your church?
Pastors and elders: what's *new* in
your leadership? Our job isn't to
preserve the old ways but to find
new ways to present, model, and
apply old truths.

Being transparent isn't
just admitting your faults,
it's also allowing people to
access your gifts and wisdom
when they are in need.

God doesn't get chills or tear up
when we sing old hymns.

The song says, "Let it go!" What do you need to let go of before God can fill your hands, heart, or life with something *new*?

God spoke to Mr. Noah to build the ark. Then Mr. Noah had to explain it to Mrs. Noah.

"I'll get my life right and then do God's will" is foolish thinking. You will find the incentive to "get it right" *as* you pursue God's will, not before.

Hebrews 11:34b – "[W]ho became powerful *in* battle and routed foreign armies.' Sometimes you don't feel God's might until you are *in* the battle, not before.

"I don't know how I feel about what my church is doing. We don't sing enough hymns or now we changed the way we do Sunday School." Doesn't matter. It's not *your* church, it's *His* church. Your preferences are irrelevant.

Hebrews 11:30 – "By faith the walls of Jericho fell, after the army had marched around them for seven days." Thirteen times they marched around the walls before they fell; you need to finish what it is God told you to do before your walls fall as well.

Hebrews 11:23 – "By faith Moses' parents hid him for three months after he was born, because they saw he was no ordinary child." What do you see in the youth around you? Their problems or their potential in Him?

Hebrews 11:12 – "And so from this one man, and he as good as dead, came descendants as numerous as the stars in the sky." You may think it's over, but it's not over until God says it's over.

Hebrews 11:19 – "Abraham *reasoned* that God could even raise the dead." Where are you using the reasoning ability God gave you to help you walk in faith?

Don't make decisions about tomorrow based on what you have today. Make your decisions based on what you see today and trust that what you need will be there tomorrow.

Hebrews 11:15 – "If they had been thinking of the country they had left, they would have had opportunity to return." If you want to, God will allow and even help you go *back* even though He wants you to go *forward*.

God is a good, good Father, but He has some strange kids.

Jesus was never into numbers so you shouldn't be concerned if only a few see what you do. Create in faith.

I enjoy when people like my posts, but I'm really happy when they act on my posts. Faith without action is useless.

What a privilege it is to serve the Lord; you don't have to serve, you get to serve.

The taller the building, the deeper the foundation. If your preparation is taking longer than expected, it's so your impact can be greater.

The Messiah was going to be a Nazarene who was born in Bethlehem while also coming out of Egypt. None of that made sense until *after* He was born. The same is true with the end times. We only have fragments of truth that we will understand later.

If it's God's money and He has plenty more, then why don't you spend or give it?

God, expand my mind and heart to know more, love more, touch more, understand more, do more.

Jesus turned their greatest insult, "You are a partner of the devil," into a teaching opportunity. He never took insults personally. You shouldn't either.

Jesus' normal seems abnormal because our normal is sometimes subnormal.

Jesus is a friend who sticks closer than a brother. Think about what a good friend He has been to you.

Missions starts with God giving you a heart for people who don't live near you and don't look or talk like you.

Even Jesus' anger was geared toward winning His opponents to the truth. Nothing He did was selfish or self-centered.

Jesus loved His enemies, so when He asks us to do the same, He isn't asking us to do something He was/is not willing to do.

Jesus showed that life comes through death, that rising up is achieved by going down, that getting stems from giving.

Ecclesiastes 11:4 — "Whoever watches the wind will not plant; whoever looks at the clouds will not reap." *God, I will sow this week whether conditions are right or not, whether I feel like it or not.*

I've consistently underestimated how much and how long I would have to sow to reap a harvest. There's a reason Paul wrote, "Let us not become weary in doing good, for at the proper time we will reap a harvest if we do not give up" (Galatians 6:9), for it's easy to grow weary.

God, show me things this week that will take my breath away.

Don't expect Christian behavior from non-Christians; it's hard enough to find in Christians.

God wants you to know His will, otherwise how can you be expected to do it?

Sometimes our disappointment comes from expectations of others fulfilling a need only God can meet.

The Jews had great disdain for Samaritans and Gentiles, but Jesus sent His people to them. God may also send you to minister to people you don't like — perhaps even supporters of another political party.

Your gift may not be universal; it may only be for specific people or situations. You must find where and who they are, and then go there.

"The end is near!" For me, it's one day nearer than it was yesterday. That's why I must make the most of today.

If I see it, I must not assume others do too. That's why when I see it, I must share or do it.

If you're surrounded by people who think, look, talk, vote, or act like you, you don't need God's grace to love them. *That's* why you need to expand your world.

Olympic diving judges sit where it's warm and dry to judge the performance of the divers who are cold and wet; sounds like some churches to me.

Psalm 105:16-17 – "He [God] called down famine on the land and destroyed all their supplies of food; and he sent a man before them — Joseph, sold as a slave." God can use extreme means to get you where you need to be.

God, let's make beautiful music together this week. You sing lead and I'll be the backup.

The Bible starts in a Garden but ends in a city. God wanted man to build not tend, to establish something great, not maintain something small.

No braver thing to do
than to be yourself when
everyone around you wants you
to be someone else.

Your honesty before God
isn't for His benefit,
it's for yours.
He already knows.

God won't change you into the
person you're pretending to be.
Be honest as to who you
really are and *then* He will
transform you.

When you talk to God,
you don't have to say His
name every 3rd or 4th word.
Just be real — and don't
forget to listen, too.

The cross isn't an inconvenience.
It's a process of dying to self and
being raised into newness of life.

"It's not the right season or time"
is an excuse, an expression of
your perfectionism. *This* is the
day the Lord has made.
Get busy.

You don't need a sign.
You already have one.
If God can raise the dead,
He can help you as you
go, act, and do.

God has a big book and a sharp
pencil and He *never* forgets
what you do for Him or others.
Just ask Mordecai.

'What's your purpose?'
"Well, I sort of think that it is
maybe, you know, to like
kind of help people."
Time to overcome fear
and get clear.

US$9 trillion in circulation
and God can't give you
some of it to do His will?
Be it done unto you . . .

Pray bold prayers,
expect bold answers.
No time for now-I-lay-me-
down-to-sleep petitions.

You play your note, I'll play
mine, and we'll follow the lead
of the great Conductor to make
beautiful music together!

Even the Jews separated themselves into the superior and less so; a result of the Fall is for all of us to dominate or segregate.

A coach can't get out of you what God didn't put in you. Focus on your gifts, not a list of what you wish you had.

Some need applause, others stay behind the scenes, but all must do what they do for Him and not for notoriety or selfish privacy.

'Well-rounded individual' is another term for those who are spiritually plump but out of shape; God wants you lean and mean. (Well, maybe not mean, but definitely focused).

Your gifts aren't yours to rent out to the highest bidder; they're to be used to build His kingdom under His direction.

Revelation 14:1 — "[W]ho had his name and his Father's name written on their foreheads." Why are we so concerned with the mark of the beast when we have His name written there?

Lord, convert some of our political zeal into missionary fervor.

Whenever you read this, stop what you're doing and take a praise/thanks break. "Thank You, Lord! Praise You, God!"

No matter how gifted, there's always someone more gifted than you; no matter how needy, there's always someone needier than you.

"I don't want to get ahead of the Lord." Yes, you will *really* anger God if you help too many orphans or write too many poems or do too much good.

If you can do something that will help others, why are you sitting on it, then wondering why you're depressed or anxious?

Make sure you're running the race and not just running in place.

Maturity is getting past who we think God is or want Him to be to worship Him in the truth of who He is.

Reading how David killed Goliath is nice but using it as the incentive to go kill your own giants is better.

The Bible never makes a case for the existence of God; it takes His existence for granted. That's a good starting point.

This week, God, empower me to empower others.

God has nothing to prove to you but you have something to prove to God. Can you run the race and finish the course?

God, this week let me write a little better, see a little better, love a little better.

76

Lord, show me this week where my thinking, attitudes, and habits limit Your will for my life.

My fear isn't getting ahead of the Lord, but of lagging too far behind.

Where you work didn't hire you, can't fire you, and they don't pay you. Your God takes care of all that.

Moses was curious so he went to the burning bush. *Then* God spoke to him. God will use your curiosities to guide you.

A bird doesn't sing because it has a contract, audience, or agent. A bird sings because it's a bird. Sing like a bird today.

When you read the account, God never spoke to David to go after Goliath. David concluded that was what he was supposed to do.

Revelation 3:15-16 — "I know your deeds, that you are neither cold nor hot. I wish you were either one or the other! So, because you are lukewarm — neither hot nor cold — I am about to spit you out of my mouth." Time to take your own temperature.

Jesus never called anyone to a paid position with benefits. He called them to follow Him and He promised to cover all their needs. Nothing's changed.

John was "in the Spirit" on Patmos but he knew more about what was going on in the churches than the leaders in those churches. Maybe it's time to have someone else evaluate your spiritual health, or that of your church.

God provided for His people through a raven, quail, manna, two fish and five loaves, and a jar of oil. What do you have that God can use to meet your need?

Solomon collected wives like stamps or coins. Either he was a sex addict or a control freak. Either way, his great wisdom didn't keep him from great moral failure. There's a lesson in that for modern leaders.

There's no hole or cave too deep or dark where you can hide from God.

When I was a church pastor, I told the people I was only a member who happened to have a more public gift. I was no one special.

Revelation 12:11 – "They triumphed over him by the blood of the Lamb and by the word of their testimony." Tell your story.

The day you demand honor for your role in the Kingdom is the day you have left the Kingdom to build your own.

If talk is cheap, then it's no wonder you're "broke." Less talk, more walk.

What if *you* are a stone God wants to put in His sling and toss at a giant near or far away?

Hebrews 5:11 – "We have much to say about this, but it is hard to make it clear to you because you no longer try to understand." Are you trying or complying?

"Experience is simply
the name we give our mistakes."
— Oscar Wilde

God won't give you all the
information you need to know
before you step out but *as* you
step out. Time to step out.

You pray for money,
but often God gives you
an idea you can then redeem
for cash by following through.

The four lepers asked each other,
"Why sit we here until we die?"
From one leper to another,
I ask you the same question.

When God gives you a new role,
friends who knew you in your
old one may not recognize or
like the new you. The answer
isn't to revert to the old you but
to find new friends.

If you want God to move,
you do understand that it means
you will have to "move" too?

Where and when did we begin to confuse holding "services" with actual "service"?

Expand my reach this week, Lord, along with my ability to handle it.

The Holy Spirit was sent to *lead* and *guide*, which sounds to me like He wants to take us somewhere, not leave us where He found us.

God wants to show off the new you He has created you to be.

My strategy isn't to boycott or ignore social media but to *redeem* it.

This week, Lord, I need to be more God conscious and less self-conscious.

Maturity means you're
willing to be misunderstood
so God can eventually be
better understood by others.

If you learn more from
failure than success,
then can't your failures actually
be considered a success?

The way up is down,
the way to have is to give,
the way to live is to die.
All that's true so your victory
or breakthrough will be His
and not due to your efforts.

Two pages per day in any month
and you will have written 60
pages. The problem isn't time,
it's your fear you can't produce
those pages — or that
they're not very good.

If you have been fruitful,
God will prune you so you can
bear more fruit. Don't mistake
His pruning for His displeasure.

Don't write a book, be an author.
One book isn't enough to
contain who you are,
what you know, or what
God has done in your life.

You have a purpose:
something for you to do
only you can do, something to
be only you can be.

Proverbs 28:1 —
"The righteous are as
bold as a lion."
Are you?

God can't expect you to do
His will unless you know it.
Ask in faith and then watch
and listen for the answer.

Seldom do our
idols replace God;
instead, we worship them
along with God.

God "programmed" you with
joy to help you know
when you're doing His will.
Don't run from your joy,
follow it.

There should be no trace
of bitterness or salt but
otherwise the rivers of living
water flowing from you should
taste *like you* — your gifts,
perspective, experience.

Your greatest test may not be how you handle failure but rather how you handle success.

In five minutes, Genesis Joseph went from the dungeon to the palace — and never left. Stay ready.

God never apologizes for your trials, but He always goes through them with you.

For thirteen years, Joseph served others; for 80 years after that, others served him. Serving was his training for reigning; it's yours, too.

"God, I will do *whatever* You want, as long as it's in this country, in this state, in this city, in this neighborhood, in this church on Sunday or Wednesday, among people who look or think like me — but I will do *whatever* You want."

God made Joseph fruitful in a foreign land — God may want to do the same for you.

You don't pick
where you will blossom;
He does.

Ruth's story proves that
God honors loyalty.

Joseph's brothers didn't just hate
him; they tried to kill him, but
instead sold him for profit. Your
enemies not only oppose your
purpose but also confirm it.

Be faithful where you are and
with what you have, and God
will give you more — money,
responsibility, followers, friends.

Joseph was misrepresented, lied
to, forgotten, betrayed, oppressed,
used, and enslaved. Thirteen years
later, he received the "Master's"
degree in administration with a
significant promotion. God knows
what He's doing.

Daniel proves even hungry lions
can't harm you when God
shuts their mouths.

Be you;
everyone else is taken.

Too often I haven't done or
given the little I could because
it wasn't a lot; don't judge your
good deeds by their size or
impact, just do them.

God isn't deaf,
so there's no need to shout.

The song says,
"What's love got to do with it?"
God's response is: "Everything."

Volume does *not* make your
prayer more effective —
only faith does.

Sometimes our faith has to be
in the fact that God is love,
even when things happen that
seem to contradict that.

Revelation 3:16 — "Because you are lukewarm — neither hot nor cold — I am about to spit you out of my mouth." God isn't impressed with half-hearted service.

Mark 10:45 — "For even the Son of Man did not come to be served, but to serve, and to give his life as a ransom for many." We don't believe that leadership is best expressed in service, which is why we have so many leaders who dominate and control.

Anointed teachers study so God has something to anoint.

Rather than being taught, isn't it time you stepped up and did the teaching?

Genesis 3:16 — "Your desire will be for your husband, and he will rule over you." Our drive to dominate others is part of our fallen nature.

If you're out of spiritual shape, even the shortest faith walk leaves you short of breath.

JOHN W. STANKO

87

Whining is the opposite of praise, grumbling the opposite of thanksgiving.

James 4:7 — "Submit yourselves to God. Resist the devil, and he will flee from you." You can't be passive and expect to grow in the Lord.

God, may I not consume or waste Your presence but use it as fuel to carry out my purpose assignment.

When you stand before the Lord, He will not want to know how many church services you attended.

Psalm 31:14-15 — "But I trust in you, Lord; I say, 'You are my God.' My times are in your hands."

God isn't interested in helping you manage your little world but in expanding your capacity to help tend His big world.

You must still have purpose;
you're still here.

Where do you see yourself in
two years? five? ten?
If you don't know where
you're headed, then any road
(or no road) will do.

Faith isn't a parachute you
use in an emergency;
it's the oxygen tank
you wear all day.

The same Spirit that raised
Christ from the dead dwells in
you! What are you doing with
that latent power?

John 17:4 — "I have brought you
glory on earth by finishing the
work you gave me to do." Jesus
glorified the Father by fulfilling
His purpose, not by saying,
"Glory to God" or singing a song.
You should do the same.

"Less of me, more of You"
sounds good, but if people
are going to see more of Him
through You, they must see
more of you in Him.

Jesus doesn't need you to take Him to church; He's already there. He needs you to take Him to places where He isn't.

God will lead you to an opportunity and may ask you, "What do *you* want to do with this?"

When you go somewhere, it's polite to introduce others to Jesus who's there along with you.

Deciding not to decide *is* a decision and it has implications.

A sign isn't for believers, but unbelievers. Requests for repeated confirmations indicate fear, not maturity.

If God can do exceedingly abundantly beyond all you can ask, think, or imagine, then how can you get ahead of Him?

If God knows your thoughts from afar, then why would He be angered when you are honest with Him? If He were going to "get" you, wouldn't He "get" you for thinking it before you say it?

What you expect to see you will probably see, so in a sense, you have a say in what you see.

You are surrounded by a great "cloud of witnesses" according to Hebrews 12:1-2. Put on a good show for them today.

I read somewhere that a friend is someone who when you make a fool of yourself, doesn't believe it's a permanent condition.

Perhaps more than a to-do list you need a *stop* to-do list.

The higher your call, the deeper and longer your preparation.

You have what you need
for today; don't worry that
what you need tomorrow
won't be there.
It will.

"God will make a way where
there seems to be no way"
aren't just the words to a song,
it's a slogan summarizing
a way of life.

You learn to make
good decisions by making
some bad ones.

The Spirit is in you to give you
the mind of Christ so you can
think the very thoughts of God.

You won't know
how far you can go
until you risk
going too far.

Going where you're celebrated
and not just tolerated is God's
way of guiding you to where
you need to be.

You don't have to swim, boat,
or surf across your Red Sea;
God will part the waters
so you can walk through.

God is seldom early, never late,
but He's always on time. Sounds
good, huh? So what deadlines
have you set for His arrival?

You "can" do all things is nothing
but a statement of potential until
you do some of the all things
you claim you can do.

God will never ask
any more of you
than He knows
you can give.

You want to commit once you
have the resources;
God would have you commit
before you have them and trust
Him to bring them.

*Lord, I want to enjoy
Your presence this week and
go with the flow.*

If you help one person, that's good, but if you could have helped 100 but only helped one, it's irresponsible.

When Goliath came toward David, David *ran* toward him, loading his slingshot while he went. Time to meet your giants head on with courage.

You aren't even guaranteed the rest of today so make the most of every moment.

God cannot promote your potential unless you first develop it.

God, breathe on my work so it will go farther and touch more.

Some of Jesus' parables speak to God's expectation of increase wherever He plants you. To simply maintain is not enough.

Psalm 98:1 — "Sing to the Lord a new song." A new melody, new lyrics, new harmonies — they all require you to *change your tune*.

While I wait for my "best seller," I keep writing books. In other words, while I wait, I act.

1 Corinthians 15:58 — "Let nothing move you. Always give yourselves fully to the work of the Lord, because you know that your labor in the Lord is not in vain."

What if my "best seller" emerges after I'm gone? That's why I write in faith.

Treat all your ideas as royalty, for one of them may be king.

Hebrews 11:39 — "These were all commended for their faith, yet none of them received what had been promised." I've determined I would rather die in faith than live in fear.

Jesus knew how dangerous power is, which is why He said we can't lead like the Gentiles, but must serve like the youngest. We don't believe that's possible, lead *and* serve that is.

Matthew 6:33 – "But *seek first his kingdom and his righteousness, and all these things* will be *given* to you as well." *All these things* are your food, clothing, and transportation and they are a gift; you do *not* work to earn them.

Don't talk yourself into fear and fatigue; talk yourself out of them into courage and strength.

You don't work to make money. You work to extend God's Kingdom where He places you. The money is His provision and if you allow Him, He can provide for you beyond your salary.

Jonah proves God's whale is bigger and faster than your getaway ship.

Your company didn't hire you, can't fire you, and doesn't pay you. You don't serve it, you serve *Him* by serving it. Thus, He is your career counselor and agent.

Colossians 3:23-24 — "Whatever you do, work at it with all your heart, as working for the Lord, not for human masters, since you know that you will receive an inheritance from the Lord as a reward. It is the Lord Christ you are serving."

Don't set up a false standard and portray it as God's. God expects nothing from you except to be who He created you to be.

Genesis 1:29 — "Then God said, 'I *give* you every seed-bearing plant on the face of the whole earth and every tree that has fruit with seed in it. They will be yours for food.'" Your food is a gift, *not* a result of work. You don't work for Pharaoh, you work for Him.

"Someone needs to do something." If you can see what needs to be done, then that someone may be *you.*

If you don't get control of your thought life, you won't rest even when you rest.

Arrogance is believing what you see and know is all there is to see and know.

Speaking the truth in love means love is the motivation to speak, not the need to be correct or to correct.

Your testimony is not yours until you share it, and then it becomes community property.

If bullying others is wrong, then so is bullying yourself. Learn to do things because you *want* to not because you *have* to.

When you mess up, don't run *from* God, run *to* Him.

Faith is not a pill you swallow when you're in need, but rather spiritual vitamins you take every day.

The Cross set me free to be who God made me to be, not who I thought I was to be, not who others said I was to be.

The Cross paved the way
for Pentecost through
the Resurrection. I have
all the power I need to
live out God's will.

To know God is to take
your problems to Him,
expecting Him to show you the
solutions; that's called faith.

Jesus came to restore *all* things
to their Garden condition
before the Fall, not in the
by-and-by, but *now*.

Jesus worked hard on
the Sabbath, but it was
purpose work that always
gives more than it takes.

Yes, the heart is wicked,
but guess what? God has given
you a new heart! You can trust
it more than you have been
led to believe.

Proverbs 17:6 –
"Grandchildren are the
crowning glory of the aged."
Ask me how I know
that to be true.

Sometimes when God wants to speak to you, He takes you on a trip to get you away from the familiar so you are more in tune with your need for Him.

When you appear before the Lord, He won't ask what church you were in but what Kingdom you were in.

It's futile to say you're going to do something grandiose when you can't keep a small promise of what you're going to do today.

Why the struggle? Jesus said His yoke is easy and burden light. If you're carrying something heavy, it may not be His yoke or burden.

You're waiting for your circumstances to change before you act. Could it be that they will change only *when* you act?

Faith is like flying a plane in fog. You can't always see where you're going but your faith GPS tells you you're heading in the right direction.

Following God
can't be a hobby,
it must be
your main occupation.

God wants to use your five
loaves and two fish to feed
others instead of you always
looking to eat theirs.

You can't steal second base
while holding your foot on first.
Time to take off and run.

I'm not sure why when we
have the good news that we
spend so much time watching
reports of the bad news.

"I have a book or a business
or a ministry on my heart."
It's not doing anyone any good
as long as it stays there.

God's less interested in
you commemorating the
resurrection than He is in you
living the resurrection.

The only "race"
I am interested in
is running the one
God has set before me.

Since our Garden Fall, *every*
people group, regardless of skin
color, has looked for another
group to oppress. If we are going
to go back in history to deal with
this problem, we have to go
all the way back.

My nation has turned from God
and looks to Washington DC
for help. And we wonder why
we have the problems we do.

Diversity should be about
celebrating God's multifaceted
creation, not exalting evil.

When a nation calls the ugly
beautiful, the wrong right,
the profane noble, the righteous
evil, the good bad, the bad good,
they can expect Hosea 8:7:
"They sow the wind and
reap the whirlwind."

Keep in mind that while
I need those who do not look
or think like me, they also need
me — we are in this together.

Exodus 13:13 — "But every firstborn of a donkey you shall redeem with a lamb; and if you will not redeem it, then you shall break its neck." Lesson: Don't be a donkey in the things of God.

All of us are smarter than one of us, but only if all of us have some sense to begin with.

The day I can't say something is evil for fear of offending *either* political party is the day I have surrendered my ordination.

Your job isn't to try and find out what's going to happen in the future, it's to work with God to make something happen in the future.

Heavenly beings don't stand or kneel when the National Anthem is played; they have their own music.

What's your active faith-project that if God doesn't come through, you will look foolish?

If God will meet all your needs, then create more need (for wisdom, His presence, direction, provision, knowledge).

What looks like chaos to you doesn't to Him, so stop trying to control things and let Him help you find your way through.

No more now-I-lay-me-down-to-sleep prayers; it's time to talk to God as your Father and allow Him to talk to you as His mature child.

You are only too old or too young if you think you are.

You can lean on God; He won't bend or break.

If we learn more from failure than success, then you should have earned a doctorate right about now.

We have so pigged out on doctrine that we need a vigorous regimen of good deeds to lose some theological weight.

"Not all those who wander are lost."
— J.R.R. Tolkien

You don't work for pay, you work to extend God's Kingdom rule where you are and the King takes care of your needs.

Jesus came to reconcile *all* things to the Father, including your purpose, creativity, and personality.

God supplies all your needs, so if you are having a difficulty, it must be because you need what it will teach you.

Hebrews 7:25 (NKJV) — "Therefore He is also able to save to the *uttermost* those who come to God through Him, since He always lives to make intercession for them." *You* are saved to the *uttermost*.

Proverbs 14:34 (NLT) —
"Godliness makes
a nation great, but sin is
a disgrace to any people."

*If riding the bench will
help Your team win, Lord,
then I will ride it like it has
never been ridden before.*

*Lord, this week I want to be
better at what I do than last
week. Empower me, I pray.*

You don't know the
upside of your potential
until you start to develop it.

*God, if You want me to sing
harmony or backup for someone
else's solo, I'm happy to do so.*

Two ears plus
one mouth equals
listening twice as much
as you talk.

Don't try to be
more than you are,
but for God's sake,
don't be any less either.

If you aren't happy
with what you're reaping,
perhaps it's time to
examine what you're sowing.

Proverbs 11:26 – "People curse
the one who hoards grain,
but they pray God's blessing
on the one who is willing to
sell." Don't hoard your gifts or
creativity; find ways to share
them with others.

We often pursue "normal" but
don't really know what it is or
looks like. Your normal is you
being true to who God made
you to be.

John 1:11 – "He came to that
which was his own, but his own
did not receive him." Are you
willing to be rejected by your
family, your race, or your people
and take a stand for God?
Don't answer too quickly.

If your focus is on your needs,
you won't see the needs of
others. And serving the needs
of others is often how God
meets yours.

God's less interested in changing your circumstances than He is in changing how you see and evaluate them.

Maturity is thinking about how you can share with others the lessons from your toughest times.

Empathy is feeling what others feel without them telling you how they feel.

We should all minister like Jesus: "People were overwhelmed with amazement. 'He has done everything well'" — Mark 7:37.

Sometimes the less you feel God's presence, the more faith you need in His invisible and loving hand of guidance.

Sometimes people who want you to be balanced don't want you to exceed what they can do.

Jesus knows what it's like to be an oppressed minority treated with cruelty. He responded with love and forgiveness.

Jesus didn't have to go to the cross, He chose to go there

Be careful when you demand justice for if God were just with you, where would you be?

John 12:32-33 — "'And I, when I am lifted up from the earth, will draw all people to myself.' He said this to indicate the kind of death He was going to die."

The cross isn't one of many ways to God, it's the only way.

The choice is clear and still being made: either the insurrectionist/murderer Barabbas or the Prince of Peace.

The Jews regularly demonstrated against Rome; people were often killed, and a strong security presence was required to keep the peace. Sound familiar?

The Cross is the vaccination that once accepted by faith is the inoculation against sin.

Jesus chose a hated tax collector, conservative Jews, small businessmen, and a right-wing zealot to be in His cabinet. And He had a group of women traveling with them all. I'm sure they all got along with no tension.

Lord, empower me to fulfill the opportunities You have for me this week.

The Pharisees proved the group that opposes the current move of God is often the group from the last move of God.

Lord, I can only do more if You expand my capacity to love, know, care, act. I'm willing.

God, I know somehow and in some way my thinking is blocking my ability to do more. Give me new thoughts.

God, if I'm going to touch more, I have to be more. The limit isn't in You, it's in me.

There's no way I'm capable of doing what's before me, Lord. That's why I'm confident I'm on the right path.

God isn't that interested in preserving your way of life but in getting you to embrace His way to life.

When Jesus rose, He began a 40-day intensive with His disciples. We know what He taught them because they shared it with us through the Word.

Don't give because God will bless you, but when you give, God will bless you.

You'll only do what you can do when you stop trying to do what you can't do.

God doesn't owe you an audience; you have to earn that through excellence, consistency, and meeting people's needs.

Sincerity is no substitute for accuracy or action. You can be sincere but sincerely wrong — or sincerely lazy.

We often overestimate the impact of our failures and underestimate the potential of our success.

You can have a green light and hit someone crossing against the light, which means being in the right shouldn't always be the highest priority.

Pay a bill, send a gift, make a repair, send flowers; take someone's breath away today with an unexpected good deed.

God isn't looking for connoisseurs of ministry, He's looking for producers of ministry. Don't judge, *do*!

What promises did you make to the Lord during the pandemic? Time to pay up and follow through.

"What if my idea doesn't work?" But what if it does?

Sometimes the testimony you don't want to give is the testimony you *need* to give.

We agonize over the wrong we do but seldom over the good we didn't do.

The cross is more than the declaration you wear around your neck. It should be a burden you carry around your heart.

Don't use the best of
your creativity to
manufacture excuses.

Waiting for a confirmation of
God's will, while commendable,
is actually a lack of faith, not
evidence of it.

What could you do today
and every day thereafter if
you weren't afraid?

You do *not* have the
last job in the universe.
It's not the end of the world
to find a new one. Better yet,
start your own business.

I'm confident it's not God's will
that you wake up every morning
and dread doing the job you
have. Find the work you love.

Your enemies don't show up
until you find your purpose.
Just ask David, Paul, Jesus,
or Joseph. The opposition
confirms you're doing
something right, not that you
have missed the Lord.

Philippians 3:18 – "*Many* live as enemies of the cross of Christ." Paul was *not* writing about unbelievers.

We exist not for our own sake, but for the sake of others, especially those who don't know Him.

Revelation tells us that Babylon is the mother of harlots who sell who they are and what they have for money. The Kingdom is the mother of servants who do what they do for the love of God and others.

The church exists not to entertain the saints but to find and make new ones.

No matter where God sends you, He'll be there when you arrive and be your companion along the way.

The church isn't a convenience store but a petrol station for the long journey ahead.

Babylon is seldom
against God; they just make
Him one among many.
We live in modern Babylon.

With revelation comes
responsibility. Don't seek the
Lord for insight unless you're
ready to do something with it.

Jesus didn't need a sound system
to teach; He only needed
an opportunity.

The world can only find God
through His people.

Thus asketh the Lord,
"What part of G-O
don't you understand?"

We are to use bushels to
carry our fruit, not to cover
who we are or what
God is doing in our lives.

We aren't only to teach the truth, but also to model the truth.

God, breathe on my words, give them life, and carry them to those who need them most.

If you want to create interesting things, you must do interesting things.

Deuteronomy 8:3 – "He humbled you, causing you to hunger and then feeding you with manna." God will put you in a desert and then provide for you in ways you can't take credit for.

So many things to do and ways to go this week, Lord. I need Your wisdom to establish and follow Your priorities.

Don't put God in a box. He isn't limited to provide for you through where you work.

The best way to get a word from the Word when you need a word is to be in the Word when you don't need a word.

Today is the past of your future, so if you want good memories, make the most of this day.

If God reveals the future to you, it's not so you can be in the know, but so you can prepare now for your role then.

Boredom is God's way of telling you it's time to move on. Don't learn to live with it.

If you set a goal to lose two pounds by December 31 and it's January 10, it's not a goal; it's a delay tactic. Think of your goals in terms of ASAP and now.

I'm confident you're capable of doing more than you are, but are you willing?

Your job isn't to shrink your world to its most manageable size so you don't need God's help, but to expand it to where you can't manage it without His help.

Joshua 3:4 — "Then you will *know* which way to go, since you have never been this way before." God doesn't want you to stick to the ways you know; He wants to take you on a new journey.

If you want to be good at something, usually you have to be willing to be bad at it for a while.

John 13:17 — "Now that you know these things, you will be blessed if you do them." God wants you to know so you can *do*, not just so you can know.

If you want to do more, then you must learn more. If you want more of God, then you must learn more about Him and His ways.

God wants you to "play the martyr" because the word *martyr* means witness.

If God asked you to gather your fruit and bring it to Him for inspection, what would You bring Him?

When you play small, you deprive the world of your unique contribution and dishonor God.

God doesn't want nice people. He wants nice *productive* people.

At his coronation, King Saul was found hiding in the baggage. Don't hide in the baggage of your fears like he did.

Faith isn't an event, it's a lifestyle. It isn't a last resort, it's a first response.

Jesus was more annoyed by the disciples' lack of faith than He was by the storm.

One minute Joseph was in the dungeon and the next he was vice-president of the most powerful nation on earth. God can promote you in an instant and not follow any rules or protocols.

God's will for Daniel was for him to serve his oppressors. So, who was really in charge, the Babylonians or God's man?

Esther was an orphan but then was selected to be the queen. Your destiny's in God's hands and isn't based on your circumstances.

What commitments did you vow you would keep after the pandemic was over? Are you following through or wavering?

After Esther was chosen, she was sent to beauty school for one year to become more of who she already was. God wants to do the same for you — help you be more of who you already are, that is.

The Dead Sea is dead not because it lacks nutrients but because it has an abundance of them with no outlet. Don't be a Dead Sea believer.

We are the best-educated and best-resourced generation in the history of the Church. To whom much is given, much is required.

Lord, I'm grateful for 72 years of life and dedicate the next year to Your service.

If a church or individual isn't growing, they are in decline. How do you measure your growth to ensure you're on the right path?

Your purpose makes you like the burning bush; you will burn brightly, drawing the attention of others, but will never burn out.

With God, good enough seldom is.

God's more comfortable with your humanity than you are. Stop trying to change things and learn to be yourself.

Lord, I strive this week to be a better friend, a better counselor, a better coach, a better writer.

God, I don't want to have an ordinary year, but rather an extraordinary one in You and Your service.

I want to be used up when I die and there be nothing left because I wrote it all, read it all, said it all, traveled it all.

David fought the bear and the lion and then he took on Goliath. Your private victories today set the stage for tomorrow's public success.

God, for my birthday, I don't want to receive gifts, I want to use my gifts to bestow gifts.

I write,
God provides the readers.
You do your part and
God will do His.
You don't, He won't.

If God is the light in your life,
it's time for you to
take the cover off and let Him
shine through you.

Success is doing what you love
as often as possible;
money is a byproduct
not a destination.

"I'm too busy" is a convenient
excuse to cover fear;
the simple solution is to
get un-busy.

You have a purpose,
something to do only
you can do, something to be
only you can be.

Ecclesiasticus 11:25 —
"Hardship is forgotten in
time of success and
success in time of hardship."

Your purpose isn't to do no
wrong, but to do as much right
for others as you possibly can.

God will seldom provide for your needs in the way you think He will and then will seldom provide the same way twice.

On a plane, they call for anyone in medicine to help a sick passenger. Imagine if a doctor or nurse thought, "I don't want to draw attention to myself" and remained silent. Same is true for your purpose. People need you; this is no time for false humility.

God doesn't need your permission to use you as He sees fit; He just needs your cooperation.

No matter the wrong you suffered, you are to respond in a Kingdom way and not in a culturally-acceptable way.

You lost your right to privacy the day you gave your life to Jesus; on that day, you became public property.

Idolatry isn't replacing God with other gods, it's worshiping those gods along with Jehovah God.

We're to be a peculiar people, not with eccentric personalities, but with unique, non-self-centered actions.

Isaiah 8:12-13 — "Do not call conspiracy everything this people calls a conspiracy; do not fear what they fear, and do not dread it. The Lord Almighty is the one you are to regard as holy, he is the one you are to fear, he is the one you are to dread."

The gravitational pull of your culture, white, Black, or any other, is powerful, and only a Kingdom mindset can set you free.

Revelation 12:15 — "Then from his mouth the serpent spewed water like a river, to overtake the woman and sweep her away with the torrent." The woman is the church, and she's still the serpent's enemy with whom he wars.

Speaking of staying woke: Ephesians 5:14-15 — "This is why it is said: 'Wake up, sleeper, rise from the dead, and Christ will shine on you.' Be very careful, then, how you live."

God isn't a passive God and therefore isn't looking for a passive people. He's active doing good and expects us to do the same.

We must address the ills of society without being consumed by those ills — or our anger.

If grace is undeserved merit and we have received it, why are we sometimes so hesitant to dispense it to undeserving people?

Love is always the right strategy.

Grace, forgiveness, love, reconciliation are unique characteristics of believers. They don't indicate we're soft, they show we're obedient.

The world expects to see two things in the Church: love and care for the poor. Interesting they know what many in the Church have ignored or forgotten.

We aren't to be consumers of the Word but rather doers of the Word.

There are those who do and those who judge what others do. I think God has called us to the former.

One-tenth of what you earn doesn't belong to God, ten-tenths of it does.

Balance is often a place and concept to which we retreat when we're afraid we're going too far.

I'm a church member because I'm a Kingdom citizen; the Kingdom is the priority.

God has put all His resources at your disposal. Have you done the same with yours to Him?

When someone gives you a gift, you may eventually reciprocate. Shouldn't you do the same with God's gifts and give something back to Him?

Lord, this week will present unprecedented opportunities. Help me see and seize them.

1 Thessalonians 5:16-18 — "Rejoice always, pray continually, give thanks in all circumstances; for this is God's will for you in Christ Jesus."

Lord, let my source of stability be in You and not my attempts to keep this week pretty much the same as the last one.

Matthew 5:9 — "Blessed are the peacemakers, for they will be called children of God." Our job isn't to contribute to chaos or stir the pot of anger, but to find ways to speak and act that lead to peace and harmony.

"Work from early till late. In fact, I have so much to do that I shall spend the first three hours in prayer." — Martin Luther

Churches should be like spiritual AAA 24/7 roadside assistance, but instead we are open for business two or three hours maximum two days a week.

God is often in the interruptions, shaking our complacency and challenging our self-satisfaction with the status quo.

Maturity is unlearning what you previously learned that's now hindering you from maturing.

Revelation 21:4b-5 — "'For the old order of things has passed away.' He who was seated on the throne said, 'I am making everything new!'" That means change is coming!

John 7:38 — "Whoever believes in me, as Scripture has said, rivers of living water will flow from within them." Does a river of living water flow from you? What does it taste like? Look like? Can others drink it?

What you need tomorrow will be there. Thank God for what you have today.
The higher your calling, the deeper your preparation.

Jesus said we can't serve God and mammon or riches;
He didn't say riches are bad, but serving them is.

As in the Garden,
God directs our work,
but expects us to involve
our purpose and creativity
to get the job done.

God isn't only Lord of
your prophecy but also
Lord of how it will be fulfilled.

I don't put my faith in
my ability to hear the Lord, but
rather in His ability
to get through to me.

Your purpose is like clothing
bought too big for a child;
God fully expects you will
grow into it.

If the disciples misunderstood
and needed clarity and they
were sitting right next to Jesus,
you can be sure we will need
clarity as well.

*God, help me feel what others
feel who have messed up,
given up, shut up, spoken up,
and broken up so I can help
them rise up.*

Time to share some of those journals you have written so others can benefit from your journey and wisdom.

My days are numbered as are yours. That's why I work fervently, frantically even, for I don't know how many I have left.

If God is invisible, but you want people to see Him, then doesn't it make sense that they must see Him *in you*?

You find time to do what's most important to you. So, if you aren't doing something, you may claim it's important — but it isn't.

When you hear the Word and say "Amen," it means "so be it" and involves making a commitment to do or be what you heard.

You're correct: If you wait long enough, you won't have to or be able to do the thing that's in your heart to do.

*God, help me not only
do right things but also do them
in the right way.*

Your testimony isn't really yours;
it belongs to other people,
and you have a duty and
need to share it.

Make sure your "I can't"
isn't really covering for your
attitude that says "I won't."

The scoreboard clock for my life is
ticking down; I can't see the time left,
but I know I'm in the fourth quarter;
that's why I make every day count.
Stop assuming you have all the time
in the world; you only have today.
Make it count.

You plus God equals a majority
and together you outnumber all
those who are against you.

God's idea of "soon" and mine
are often quite different; that's
why I need diligence to see His
promises through to completion.

Lord, I'm excited for the opportunities I have this week to serve You and others. Help me make the most of them.

In his book *The Compound Effect*, Darren Hardy wrote, "Never ask advice of someone with whom you wouldn't want to trade places."

Faith shouldn't be a last resort but a first response.

The things of God are sacred, your routine is not. Don't spend time resisting what is destined to change.

A personal prophecy or word is like an old photo negative; you play a role in its development.

As the old song says, God may not come when you call him, but He always comes on time.

Hurt people hurt people.
If you want to be a source of
healing, then allow God to heal
your own pain.

You don't have to
go looking for purpose,
it comes looking for you.

When your trial has
nothing more to teach you,
only then will it disappear.

1 Corinthians 16:9 — "Because a
great door for effective work has
opened to me, and there are many
who oppose me." Your opposition
is a confirmation not that you're
doing something wrong but that
you're doing something right.

Because you're afraid to
ask for too much,
you often ask for too little.

John 13:17 — "Now that
you know these things, you will
be blessed if you do them." What
are you doing with
what you know?

The story of Gideon proves that quality is more important to God than quantity, reliability rather than availability.

Success is learning to live off and for heaven's applause when all you hear is the world booing.

God will respond to you with the same intensity and urgency you display when you seek Him.

Psalms 50:10 — "I [the Lord] own the cattle on a thousand hills." Don't settle for a burger when you can have steak.

Philippians 2:5 — "You must have the same attitude that Christ Jesus had." Do you?

The more knowledge you have, the more God has to anoint.

Proverbs 18:10 — "The name of the Lord is a strong tower; the righteous runs into it and is safe." Are you running to God or from Him?

If you're ignorant and God anoints you, you then have anointed ignorance.

I would rather die in faith than live in presumption.

Seeking God's face means you learn to read His actions and 'facial expressions,' not just His words.

God's heart is for the nations. What are you doing to reach them for Christ?

Watch TV 30 minutes less per day and use that time to read.

"Go ye into all the world."
What part of "go"
isn't clear to you?

All the other religions blur
or destroy individuality;
Christianity depends on it,
for each person has a gift,
a song, an insight.

Boredom is God's way of telling
you it's time to move on.

Psalm 103:2 —
"Praise the Lord, my soul,
and forget not all his benefits."

*Lord, the man I was last week
isn't adequate to meet the
opportunities of this week.*

If you're desperate
for a vacation,
you're in the wrong business;
purpose always gives
more than it takes.

Sometimes the most intense opposition you face isn't from without but from within.

It's good to wait on the Lord, but once He speaks, it's time to run.

Lord, may Your power empower me this week to take advantage of the opportunities You provide.

Thomas proves that doubt isn't fatal, that faith is seldom perfect.

God doesn't rely on your self-image of who you are and what you can do when He chooses what you will be and do.

You don't have to be extraordinary; you just have to put your trust in the One who is.

God is love,
so when you do what you love,
you know you are doing the
thing God wants you to do.

*Lord, this week help me find
those who need what I have
that You have given me.*

Goliath proves the best way to
deal with an enemy is to
run right at it.

The opportunities to do good
deeds today are abundant
but you'll miss them if you're
focused on your own needs.

Jesus came not to look good,
but to do good, which is why
He looked bad to those who
only wanted to look good.

Love covers a multitude of sins
but it's easy to underestimate
the multitude of sins involved
that our love must cover.

You should have no idea how you will accomplish your faith goals, only that God will help you achieve them.

Faith is like a muscle; the more you use it, the bigger it gets.

Go where you're celebrated, not simply tolerated. It's God way of showing you where He wants you to be.

First you were too young now you say you are too old; you are running out of excuses and time.

If God used Samson, He can use anyone — even you. Your past failures don't determine your present or future effectiveness.

Don't die with your music still in you; sing your song.

By the authority vested in me
as a life purpose coach,
I give you permission to
be who God made you to be.

God wants to expand your heart
so you care for *the* world and
not just *your* world.

Psalm 119:37 — "Turn my eyes
away from worthless things;
preserve my life according to
your word."

Be yourself:
everyone else is taken.

When you consume the Word
without an outlet to apply
what you've learned, you
become an overweight believer,
addicted to receiving but
anemic toward giving.

Your generosity is
the barometer that
measures your faith.

"When things improve in my life, I will serve Him."
No, when you serve Him, things improve.

Those who minister the Word aren't a privileged class but a cadre of servants.

When God says not to fear, He's actually telling you that you're already afraid.

God, give me clarity of thought and purpose this week so I can keep the main thing the main thing.

We have assumed better theology would automatically create better leaders in the church; it has not.

Time to get off your "but" and be fruitful.

You need the benefits that come from serving and obeying the Lord more than company's benefits.

Joy is the best indicator of purpose; love is the best motivator to express it.

Your world is way too small if you only hang around with folks who look, think, and act like you.

I wish good preaching and services could help us in this hour, but they won't. What we need is bold action, not bold preaching.

When people refuse to believe or adhere to the good news, they are suckers for fake news. Don't be a sucker.

Flawed interpretations of the end times have incapacitated the church in these present times.

Waiting on the Lord isn't a passive act. It's a time when you aggressively prepare while you wait to see how and where He will use you.

God, if You open doors this week, I still have to walk through them. You do Your part and I promise to do mine.

We tend to repent for the bad things we've done, but not so much for the good things we didn't do.

God, help me be a grace dispenser and not just a grace consumer this week.

It's true: you're busy. Therefore, it may be necessary for you to stop doing some things in order to do new things.

You've prayed for money, but instead God gave you an idea; when you act on the idea, you'll have the money.

A theology of inaction uses
God as an excuse for
one's inactivity or lack of fruit.

God is a great communicator;
the problem is that I'm often
tuned in to an AM station while
He's broadcasting on FM.

If I live another ten years, I have
3,650 days left. I refuse to waste
even one of them but intend
to squeeze as much joy and
purpose into and out of each
one as possible.

Repentance isn't an event.
It's a lifestyle of being
delivered from yourself.

Singing *I Surrender All*
is the same as praying it;
what's more,
God is listening.

What are your audacious goals
that without God's help you will
never achieve? And no,
you're not too old or young to
set or achieve them.

The Pharisees prove you can memorize the Bible and still be as mean as a rattlesnake.

If God can do exceeding abundantly beyond all you can ask or think, then how can you get ahead of the Lord and do too much good?

God is here on Monday to collect on the commitments you sang on Sunday.

God doesn't owe you an audience; you have to earn that by pursuing excellence and being faithful.

When you think you deserve special treatment simply because you're the leader, you've yielded to the dark side of leadership power.

God, help me see You as You are and not as I want You to be.

God isn't punishing you; He's pruning you so you can bear more fruit for Him.

Luke 14:26 — "If anyone comes to me and does not hate father and mother, wife and children, brothers and sisters — yes, even their own life — such a person cannot be my disciple."

Colossians 1:12 — "May you be filled with joy, always thanking the Father. He has enabled you to share in the inheritance that belongs to his people, who live in the light."

Luke 14:27 — "And whoever does not carry their cross and follow me cannot be my disciple."

When people touch you in your purpose, they're touching an aspect of God He has entrusted to your care and expression.

Prayer isn't a duty, it's a privilege.

There are plenty who criticize but fewer who encourage. Determine to be one of the few.

Your past may follow you for a while, but eventually it will lose your trail and scent as God makes you into a new being.

God isn't trying to trick or trap you; He wants to set you free.

Lord, I must make every minute count this week. Help me keep my priorities straight and my faith strong.

Success is doing what you love as often as possible; money is a byproduct not a destination.

I'm not going to take God anywhere; He's already there. I'm going to serve and learn.

God has given you a gift. In many cultures, it's customary and even expected to give one back. What can you give Him?

Matthew, Mark, Luke, John, and Paul didn't get paid to write. Neither did they have a book contract. They wrote because they had something to say.

Few die from hard work, but some die from boredom and lack of purpose.

Build a church, and you often get religion; build the Kingdom and you get the church.

How will God prove He can deliver you from trouble unless He puts you in trouble and then keeps His promise?

Jeremiah 12:5 — "If you have raced with men on foot and they have worn you out, how can you compete with horses?"

Romans 8:32 — "He who did not spare his own Son, but gave him up for us all — how will he not also, along with him, graciously give us all things?' God is a giving God, and His people should be known by their generosity."

Some people need to be out front and hear the applause of others; it's not ego, it's how God made them.

God, I thank You
for Your goodness.
You treat me
better than I deserve.

If you don't give $10 when you have $100, you won't give $100 when you have $1,000; be generous now with what you have.

Israel was crying out desperately for a king while Mary was changing his diapers. God's ways are not our ways.

We're too often content with a good service that goes well rather than evaluating how well the service connects with the people.

Your faith actions create
the need for God to
move on your behalf;
no need, no move.

Matthew 2:3 –
"When King Herod heard this
he was disturbed, and all
Jerusalem with him."
God doesn't need permission
from the politicians to intervene
in the affairs of mankind.

God has never failed anyone.
Why would He spoil
a perfect record on you?

"I can do all things
through Christ" should not be
a statement of potential but
reality in your life.
What are your "all things"?

Doubt isn't just a weakness,
it's a mind disease that infects
your thoughts and speech.

It's easier to give money away
than it is to give yourself away.

The lack of courtesy, respect, and manners on social media are matched today by the attitudes and behavior of many angry drivers.

The Spirit is in you to give you the mind of Christ so you can think the thoughts of God.

I perform to please an audience of one (God) while I do what I do in front of many.

You can't keep watching, doing, reading, or thinking the same things and expect a new outcome.

A good time to leave is when you are on top, not when you are on your way down. Most leaders even in the church hold on too long.

"God, when I reap, then I promise I will sow." God says, "When you sow, then I promise you will reap."

JOHN W. STANKO

153

You don't have to be a preacher, just a witness to what you know and have seen.

God wants to show off His handiwork in you by sharing you with others.

Lord, I welcome Your royal interruptions into my busy days.

God is looking for agents, not owners; givers, not hoarders; servants, not overlords.

How can you get ahead of the Lord by doing too many good deeds? He wants you to do even more!

Service is putting who you are and all you have on the line for the betterment of others, with no expectation of a return.

Denying self also means you crucify your desire for independence and privacy to put yourself out there to meet the needs of others.

You gave your life to the Lord — you didn't loan it to Him. Therefore, He can use you as He sees fit.

Sometimes life's painful disappointments come from our expectations of others fulfilling a need only God can meet.

Islam covers personality, Buddhism obliterates it, Hinduism makes it a result of a previous life, New Age deifies it, but Christians are the only ones who accept it as an important part of God's creation to help believers fulfill their purpose.

Being transparent isn't just admitting your faults, it's also allowing people to access your gifts and wisdom all day, every day.

Philippians 2:20 — "I have *no one* else like [Timothy] who will show *genuine* concern for your welfare." *God, make me like Timothy.*

Mourning the past won't help you enter the future God is positioning you to have. Time to move on.

May my presence bring a smile to others' faces this week, Lord. Make my joy contagious.

It's better sometimes for people to think you don't know what you're talking about than to open your mouth and prove them correct.

Use what I post, say, and write this week, God, to minister to the needs of others.

Lord, help me this week to rejoice in the success of people I don't like, don't agree with, or who have wronged me.

Pain precedes promotion, dishonor before exaltation.

Smaller is not better,
bigger is not more spiritual.

You have a set of spiritual
fingerprints. When you touch
something or someone in your
purpose, you leave a mark like
no one else.

God doesn't need German
Shepherds to keep people from
Him, He needs sheepdogs who
will bring people to Him.

I don't want to watch the news,
I want to create the news.

Forget taking a leap of faith;
how about starting today
with just a step.

When you live in the past,
you're living in something
that doesn't exist—
except in your mind.

God, help me find ways this week for others to access the lessons You've taught me and the grace You've given me.

Don't use family as an excuse for why you can't do God's will right now.

Jesus wants you to transition from focusing on your deep needs to doing good deeds.

It's deception to think that all you have to do is *believe* right without having to *live* the right you believe.

You are the instrument the Lord plays to attract, inspire, instruct, or comfort others. Make sure you are in tune.

God, give me words to calm the storms in the hearts of others so they can know the peace that passes all understanding.

"Feelings lead to thinking and thinking leads to action." — Daniel Pink

Jesus may be asleep in your storm not because He doesn't care but so you can learn not to fear *before* the waves subside.

Philippians 2:13 — "For God is working in you, giving you the desire and the power to do what pleases him." God is doing His job, but you must still do the doing.

Stop waiting for the church to do *your* job or to provide a platform for *you* to fulfill *your* purpose.

Give yourself permission to be who God made you to be. No need to apologize to anyone.

God seldom gives you the resources you need until you trust Him by creating the need for those resources — before they arrive.

Two important days in your life: the day you were born and the day you find out why you were born.

God, I don't want You to fill my cup to overflowing; I want a bigger cup.

Acts 14:22 – "We must go through many hardships to enter the kingdom of God."

Some of us want overnight delivery but only have regular mail faith.

An eagle acting like a chicken would be strange. The same is true for you when you try to be less than who God made you to be.

Don't be content with getting wet or treading water in a shallow pool; it's time to swim in the ocean of your purpose.

Spiritual gluttony is consistently taking in more spiritual sustenance than you expend on your own ministry. Don't be a fat saint.

Success in the things of God isn't something you wait for, it's something you prepare for.

What I get I will give, what I hear I will say, what I think of I will do every day this week.

Lord, empower me so we can partner together to produce the kind of week You have in mind.

David was faithful in the cave and on the run, so God gave him a throne. God knows how to prepare and promote.

2 Corinthians 6:12-13 (MSG) — "The smallness you feel comes from within you. Your lives aren't small, but you're living them in a small way. Open up your lives. Live openly and expansively!"

"Christ in you, the hope of glory" means God lives in you and has access to you, but you also have access to Him!

I don't hold God responsible for the failures of His people or the church, so no need for bitterness or anger at Him— or them.

Do you have too much clutter in your life? When in doubt, throw it out. "I may need this" thinking is bogging you down with stuff.

You don't need great faith. Jesus said mustard-seed-sized faith is enough to do great things.

If you don't deal with (not ignoring or denying) your anger, your anger will deal with you.

The joy of the Lord is your strength; that's the reason you must do what you gives you joy as often as possible.

If your present path is difficult, it's not an indication you missed the Lord. It may be a confirmation you heard Him.

You haven't given enough grace to others until someone accuses you of giving too much.

Build bridges, not forts. Ask questions, don't preach. Choose service, not power.

The devil isn't your biggest problem just yet; you are your biggest problem. Get out of your own way and be fruitful.

If your advisors or mentors think and act like you, then they aren't advisors, they're your bodyguards protecting you from change.

There's unique music in you. It's time to sing your song, not hum the tune of others.

Jesus is our only model of how to respond when our rights are violated, our feelings hurt, our presence disrespected.

The rich young ruler proves God isn't after your money; He's after you.

You can love money even though you don't have any.

The Temple proves God can use a building, but He won't hesitate to tear it down when it becomes an idol.

God doesn't want more of you; He wants *all* of you — for your own good.

Luke 12:22 — "Jesus said, 'Therefore I tell you, do not worry about your life, what you will eat; or about your body, what you will wear.'" That's a command not a recommendation.

The problem with taking mental notes is that the ink fades so quickly. That's why it's best to journal and write things down.

The wrong work robs you of energy, but purpose work always replenishes what it uses.

If you're talking to God and He's not responding, then change the subject by asking new and better questions.

God comforts you with more than you need so you can give some away.

Giving isn't a spiritual lottery where you hope to hit the jackpot after your next offering.

We're called to change, not rearrange.

God can use an organization or company to pay you but He doesn't need one to do so.

It's a sign of maturity to be able to carry your own pain and that of another, and to minister to theirs in the midst of yours.

God won't tolerate in you what He seems to overlook in others; don't whine — it's part of your training for reigning.

Power concentrated in one person, whether in government, business, or church, is a dangerous thing.

"No weapon formed" actually means a *lot* of weapons will be formed and used against you — it's just that none of them will succeed.

I want to be the best purpose coach there is; the "ranking" is up to God, the preparation is up to me.

Psalm 47:7-8 – "For God is the King of all the earth; sing to him a psalm of praise. God reigns over the nations; God is seated on his holy throne."

God will show Himself strong on your behalf; will you show yourself strong on His?

My goal is not to consume ministry but to produce it, not to sell ministry but to give it away.

When God guides, He provides; when it's God's will, it's God's bill.

You may be the only Bible some people read today. Make sure you're in the New Testament of grace and not the Old Testament of judgment.

Make sure the ladder you're climbing is leaning against the right wall.

Joy isn't a luxury or optional, but a vital necessity if you want to operate in God's strength and not your own.

If the people closest to you need some of your time, it's not an interruption — it's a priority.

John 16:33 — "In this world you will have trouble. But take heart! I have overcome the world." Our reality, God's promise.

There's *no* progress without risk.

God's people exist to work; everyone else works to exist.

If you want to be an effective leader, it helps to remember what it was like to be a follower.

God is our Certainty
in uncertain times.

God has never failed you,
so why are you thinking
there's a chance that today is
the first time?

Jesus was clear: Take the beam
out of your own eye before
you try to do eye surgery on
someone else.

Once you recognize and
overcome fear,
productivity is a way of life,

There are people who want to
change the world, but can't even
remember other people's names.

Ethics begins with what you do
when the cashier gives you back
too much change.

When God wants to speak to you, He often takes you on a trip, removing you from the familiarity of your comfort zone.

Some people sell themselves for pay and benefits, only to lose their joy and sense of purpose along the way.

Rest isn't only a physical necessity, but also a mental one; you can do nothing while stressed and not be able to rest.

It's remarkable how many people feel guilty when they pursue things that give them joy.

Faith isn't an event;
it's a lifestyle.
It's not a parachute you use in emergencies,
it's a diver's air tank you learn to live through.

Some people are waiting for God to change them before He uses them; God is ready to use you as is today.

Leaders aren't remembered
for what they took,
but for how much they gave.

Some people believe when they
have sincerely said something,
they have sincerely done
something, when they have not.

Faith is the currency with which
you make spiritual transactions
with the Lord.

You read books, you read maps,
but the most important thing
you'll ever learn to
read is people.

All of us are smarter,
more spiritual,
and much more effective
than one of us.

God's looking for partners to
help create a future that glorifies
Him and develops His creation.

God neither slumbers nor sleeps,
so you can feel free to do so.

When you think you're the most
important part of the team,
you've ceased to be the most
important part of the team.

Jesus expects you to bear fruit,
not simply stay out of trouble.

If you don't know
where you're going,
any road will do.

If you wait for the
poor to knock on your door
before you do anything for
them, you'll probably
never do anything for the poor.

If you don't take care of you,
then one day others will
have to take care of you.

Humble yourself or God may have to do it for you, and that can often lead to humiliation.

You need to vaccinate yourself against greed and the only known serum to keep you safe and well is generosity.

If you can do something well but deny it for fear of appearing to be proud, then you're guilty of false humility.

Some people check their minds at the door of the church and forget to pick them up on the way out.

If you're desperate to use your time off and vacation to escape work, then perhaps you're doing the wrong work.

Just because a car is moving doesn't mean it's going in the right direction; the same is true for your organization — and for you.

Your purpose may be different than your career and only begin when your workday ends.

If a cluttered desk is a sign of a cluttered mind, as some say, then what's an empty desk the sign of?

Leaders, including pastors, should feed, even feast, on the feedback they get on their performance from their followers.

Worry isn't simply a bad habit, it's a practice that God forbids, which puts it in the category of a "sin."

Effective leaders are often measured by the ability to bear pain — their own and that of others — and still lead.

Seldom do they give you a parade or build a monument until you're gone; while you're here, you can be the target of criticism and rejection.

Are you hiding from public view because you're humble or because you've made an idol of your privacy?

Communication happens not when you speak, but when other people understand the full meaning of what you said.

Don't be fooled into thinking you'll be generous when you have a lot of money if you aren't generous when you have a little.

You can't sow corn and reap wheat; some of the lack in your life may be because you've invested your resources in one area while hoping to get results in another.

Sticking with the status quo, while seeming to be less risky, can actually be a riskier decision that moving on or out.

It requires faith to end something you can see to make room for the new things you can't yet see.

If you do what you do
for the money, even if it's
something noble and important,
the Bible calls you a hireling.

Stop trying to fix others
who don't want to be fixed.

When you serve others,
you serve God,
and God always
takes care of His servants.

"Do as I say and not as I do"
was and is always stupid advice.

God isn't trying to trick you;
He has made it simple for you to
recognize your purpose by the
joy you have when you do it.

Just because a company's
slogan is "We value people"
doesn't mean they do.

Show me a leader with a closed door, and I will show you a leader with a closed mind.

Courage isn't acting in the absence of fear but rather acting in the midst of it.

When you rest, you put your work world in God's hands and tell Him without words that you trust Him.

Worry is hard work; if you want to truly rest, you will have to confront your propensity to engage in it.

When you give yourself permission to be who you are, you release others to do the same thing.

It's an interesting phenomenon that the more Bible some people know the meaner some people get.

It's silly to talk about taking the gospel to the nations when we lack discipline to return phone calls or emails.

You'll do what you can do only when you stop trying to do what you can't do.

Your greatest test may not be how you handle failure, but how you handle success.

It's interesting how some work in miserable jobs for the health benefits, but then jeopardize their health doing work they hate.

The foundation for ethics where money is concerned is to be thankful for what you have.

A call on your life isn't restricted to church work, but relates to any position that extends God's kingdom to some aspect of His creation.

It's never a good idea to be impressed with who you are or what you can do, but always a good idea to be impressed with who God is and what He can do.

The beauty of your purpose is that you don't have to go looking for it, it will come looking for you.

If people have to tiptoe around your anger, then you have control issues that you need to confront and change.

God hates all sin — but He hates pride just a little bit more.

Football is a game played by 22 men in desperate need of rest and watched by thousands of fans in desperate need of exercise—kind of like church.

Faith isn't a parachute you put on in an emergency, but a suit of clothes you wear day in and day out,

You owe it to yourself and your family to make sure that when you leave work you leave work.

Don't give because God will bless you, but when you give, God will bless you.

People ask me all the time how I'm able to do all that I can do; my answer is that I stopped doing all the things I can't do.

Your refusal to use modern technology and social media makes you like the Amish — cute and curiously unique but culturally irrelevant.

Your values show up in two places: your checkbook and calendar. If they aren't there, then it's talk and no walk.

In the absence of specific goals, your goal then becomes to ensure that your tomorrow is just like today.

A strength leaves you feeling stronger; a weakness leaves you feeling weaker, even if you're good at performing it.

It's essential that you worship God as He is and not as you hope or wish Him to be.

It's not the people who do nothing that need encouragement the most; it's often those who are most productive.

Having fears doesn't make you less spiritual; not confronting and getting through them does.

Some leaders are spiritual arsonists. They light fires, put them out, and then remind people how important their leadership is.

The love of money doesn't have to be that you want a lot, it can simply be that you don't want to part with what you have.

Unity isn't when you
agree with one another;
it's when you agree with
the Spirit about one another.

If no one is offended by
your stand for the Lord,
then what does that say about
your stand for the Lord?

Commit to do God's will *before*
you know what it is and you
will know it when it arrives.

Your spiritual battle will be
won or lost not in the
heavenlies but in your mind.

When you go to church,
you aren't doing God a favor;
you're doing yourself a favor.

If you don't help the poor,
how else will God help the poor?

Know purpose,
know joy;
no purpose,
no joy.

You don't do good works
to get grace, you do them out
of the abundance of grace you
have already received.

God doesn't want to change you
but instead make you the fullest,
best expression of who
you already are.

Jesus doesn't want a host of
servants waiting to be told
what to do; He wants a host
of friends and disciples who
know what to do — and *do it*.

All work is good but not all work
is good for you; only the work
God assigned for you to do is
good for you.

Come to the Lord not as you
think you should be, or as others
tell you to be, or as you think He
wants you to be, but as you are.

JOHN W. STANKO

183

When you get specific with God, God will get specific with you.

Anyone can sing when things are good; can you keep singing when things are not so good?

Better not to say and do than to say and not do; better yet to say and then do.

Jesus gave His life to build His church and He expects us to do the same.

Fear is your greatest enemy where creativity is concerned; don't be surprised that you have it, just go find and confront it.

When you "see" the Kingdom, you realize that God doesn't just want to save you but to rule in every area of your life.

I don't need mercy
when I mess up, I need mercy
because I *am* messed up.

God often plays chess with you,
matching your every move;
it's your move!

I gave my life to the Lord,
I didn't loan it to Him;
what He chooses to do with it
is His business, not mine.

Your offering is generous
not based on how much you
gave according to how much
you had left after you gave.

If you don't create when you
don't have time and don't feel
like it, then you won't create
when you do have time and
you do feel like it.

None of us are getting out of
here alive, so make the most of
every day with an eye not only
on this life, but also on the
one to come.

Trust means you believe God is working on your behalf when everything looks like God isn't working on your behalf.

If you've turned a situation over to the Lord, you shouldn't take it back when you don't like how He's handling it.

God is listening; better not to promise and then do than to promise and not do.

Your biggest obstacles are not external but internal; you are often the biggest hindrance to your own success.

Your true character and faith are revealed when you have either a lot or a little.

There's no substitute for not only reading but also studying God's Word; the Holy Spirit can't do that for you.

God's word can't be a part-time interest, otherwise it will only be part-time help for your life — and you're in desperate need of full-time help.

God doesn't speak or expect King James English; He requires you to be honest with Him using your own voice and vocabulary.

No matter how much pain you're in, only God knows what you really need in the midst of it—and it may not be relief from your pain.

Mourning acknowledges your humanity, hope acknowledges God's sovereignty.

God may allow you to be lonely so you'll discover that in Him you're never alone.

When God does something for someone else, you shouldn't be envious but think, "He did it for them, He can do it for me!"

Anyone whose worship of God is a "private matter" doesn't really understand that public worship with others isn't optional.

Jesus became like you so you can become like Him.

When God wants to reveal something new to you, He often sends you on a trip.

The problem with wealth is you have to spend a lot of money to keep and protect it because it has a tendency to fly away.

Do you own your stuff or does your stuff own you?

You're part of God's family business and that business is to reach His world, not just your neighborhood, for Him.

If you didn't have any storms, you would never know God's ability to protect you in the midst of them.

Some run to the doctor for any ailment, but allow their heart wounds to fester without seeking the help of a godly counselor.

When Jesus said the gates of hell would not prevail, He didn't say they would not *try* like hell to prevail.

You can be sincere yet be sincerely wrong; that's why you must work to worship God as He is and not as you want or hope Him to be.

Maturity helps you see your critics not as your enemies but as your friends who will tell you things your friends don't have the courage to say.

Suffering and service are your tuition to attend the school of discipleship.

The more experience and
success you have,
the more difficult it can be to
trust the Lord and not your
own experience and success.

Your joy isn't to be ignored,
but trusted as a divine marker
on the road named
"God's Will for You."

Jesus may not calm your storm,
but He will walk on the water
to get to where you are.

Some capitulate and live like
the world, others retreat from
the world, but Jesus wants
you to live in and love this world
as a missionary.

Pious acts cannot erase the
stain and guilt of sin;
only asking God's forgiveness
through Christ can do that.

God loves and cares for
His creation, and expects
you to do the same.

You're never an independent contractor but a representative of Christ's body no matter where you go.

You don't need more time, you need more faith so you can fully use the time you have.

You're one event away from your breakthrough. Can you live today like it's already arrived, and be upbeat and encouraged?

If you pray to hear God's voice, then why are you surprised when He speaks?

God works through leadership but warns you not to look to receive from leadership what you can only get from Him.

When you complain, you focus on what's wrong and then won't be able to see what's right, which will only bring more wrong.

Jesus isn't interested in dating His bride; He wants a fully-committed marriage.

There are some problems you encounter that can only be explained and treated as part of the spiritual warfare common to all believers.

If you want to get God's attention, for good or not-so-good, do two things: be humble or be proud — either one is sure to evoke a response.

Your problem may not be your circumstances, but how you view them; ask God to open your eyes to see what you are not seeing.

If the Bible is God's word and reveals His will, then why do you spend so little time reading and studying it?

You save much energy and emotional torment when you mind your business and release others to the Lord, especially family.

God requires that you put aside your own needs to address the needs of others; it's called love.

God doesn't test you to see how inadequate you are but to show you and others how real and lasting His work in your life is.

Jesus came to break down gender, racial, national, class and economic boundaries between people; it's called reconciliation.

God isn't playing hard-to-get; if you truly want to know His will, He will reveal it to you

Your life story is really His-tory that you can draw on to find courage and strength to endure your day of trouble.

You didn't get saved, you're constantly being saved — from things you can see and from things you can't.

It's not enough to be like Jesus; you must also be consumed doing what Jesus did. God expects you to be childlike, but never childish.

When everything is going wrong, but you can still sleep, praise the Lord, and be generous, then you have unshakable faith.

When you say things like "I'll pray for you" or "I'll be there" and don't follow through, it's a lie, even though you were sincere when you said it.

You weren't made to drink water once a week or to fellowship with God on Sunday only; you need Him, like water, all day, every day.

Being passive is *not* a fruit of the Spirit; you must fight for the ground God has given you and not wait for Him to hand it to you.

It's good to remember that God isn't just in the business of blessing you. Therefore, rejoice when He blesses others.

God loves you too much
to leave you as you are.

It's essential that you
keep yourself right when
everything and everyone
around you is wrong.

You're never too old (or in
too much trouble) to start over
and build more intelligently
with God's help.

If God is your Father,
then Jesus is your brother
and that makes other believers
your brothers and sisters,
whether you like them or not.

Faith is making room today for
the blessings that God promises
will come tomorrow.

Don't get confused:
it's not God's job to serve you,
but your job to serve Him.

Bragging about what you can do in Christ and then doing little or nothing is *not* what God had in mind for your life.

God is neither a hot line for your complaints nor a suggestion box for your wishes, but rather an awesome focus for your praise.

Your opinions and interpretations aren't infallible and can often drown out God's corrective voice and Word.

Your hesitancy to draw attention to yourself deprives people of your testimony that they desperately need to hear.

Your body lives on three things: food, water, and air. Your spirit lives on three things: hope, faith, and mercy.

You are the bait that God uses to draw people to Him; stop playing humble and allow God to use you.

Your trials and tribulations won't last one day longer than needed to shape you into the person God wants you to be.

Life is a goal-d mine, can you dig it?

If God can feed all His creatures in nature and they don't work, He can take care of you with no problem.

Wrong thinking didn't develop in a day; it won't be overcome in a day.

The Bible keeps reminding you to trust the Lord because you tend to leak trust when the pressures of life squeeze you.

You may not live in fear only because you have made your world so small that you can easily control what you face.

God doesn't use people with potential; He uses people who have spent time developing that potential to the max.

All change takes place in the mind first, so your thinking is pivotal as you seek to do and be new things.

You are to "magnify" the Lord by taking the smallest thing He does for you and "blowing it up" so others may see it clearly.

Grace is getting what you don't deserve; mercy is not getting what you do deserve.

Jesus served and helped others who didn't return the kindness; He expects you to do the same.

God isn't a Democrat or Republican, and expects the Church to maintain its neutrality so it can prophetically speak to both.

The joy of the Lord isn't connected to what you have done, but is based on an understanding of what He has done for you.

How many confirmations will it take for you to overcome your fears and act on your ideas?

In the Christmas story, everyone was in motion—the angels, Mary, Joseph, the Magi, and the shepherds; when God "moves," you must move, too.

Mark 7:37 — "People were overwhelmed with amazement. 'He has done everything well.'" Our goal should be excellence, not mediocrity.

Maturity isn't waiting for God to do what He expects you to do, or trying to do what only He can do.

Jesus prepared His disciples for His death so they would know it wasn't a random act of violence but a purposeful act of love.

God, work through me this week and not around me.

You can't be holy 'here'
if God wants you 'there.'
Just ask Jonah.

Part of singing a new song is learning how to harmonize with others who have their own song.

Sometimes we'll take to heart the criticism of one and ignore the encouragement of ten. Not everyone is going to "get" who you are.

There's only one thing worse than waiting on the Lord, and that's wishing you had.

When you get to where God wants you to be, don't forget where you were when He found you.

Sometimes you learn to make good decisions by making a whole lot of bad ones.

Romans 12:11 — "Never be lacking in zeal, but keep your spiritual fervor, serving the Lord." How's your zeal level these days?

Jesus said if they don't receive you, shake the dust off your feet and move on. Go where you're celebrated, not tolerated.

Romans 12:16 — "Live in harmony with one another." Harmony is hard work that involves denying self.

If you insist that God judge others, be careful that He doesn't include you in the process.

Romans 12:17 — "Do not repay anyone evil for evil." The Greek word for *anyone* literally means *anyone*, even your enemies.

Romans 12:14 – "Bless those who persecute you; bless and do not curse." We're to be blessers of all people.

If you're going through hell, don't stop.

Romans 12:10 – "Be devoted to one another in love," regardless of how they vote.

Revelation proves Jesus takes on challengers and is still the Champion when the battle is over.

God's strategy hasn't changed: "Do not be overcome by evil, but overcome evil with good" (Romans 12:21).

The big lie is that you can't come to God as you are, so you come as you think you should be.

What's in your heart
comes out of your mouth —
and on social media.

God, as I prepare to travel, help
me get done what needs to be
done and entrust the rest to You.

Faith is seldom perfect,
doubt is seldom fatal.

Our job is not to expose or study
the antichrist. Our job is to
glorify and follow the Christ.

Lord, You stopped the sun for
Joshua to finish his work. I'm
trusting You for time this week
to do the same.

Don't confuse your job
with your purpose.
Your job gives you money, your
purpose gives you joy.
To combine them both is a gift.

I surrendered my right to "free speech" when I became a citizen of the Kingdom.

Grace is getting what you don't deserve; mercy is not getting what you do deserve.

The Bible reminds us to trust the Lord because we tend to leak trust when the pressures of life squeeze us.

There's no such thing as an off-duty believer.

Jesus served and helped others who did not return the kindness or express thanks; He expects us to do the same.

The fire of your trials releases the fragrant incense of His presence in your life.

About the Author

John Stanko was born in Pittsburgh, Pennsylvania and attended Duquesne University where he received his bachelor's and master's degrees in economics in 1972 and 1974 respectively.

Since then, John has served as an administrator, teacher, consultant, author, and pastor in his professional career. In 2011, he completed a doctor of ministry degree at Reformed Presbyterian Theological Seminary in Pittsburgh. John has taught extensively on the topics of time management, life purpose, and creativity, and has conducted leadership and purpose training sessions throughout the United States and in 50 countries.

John founded a personal and leadership development company, called PurposeQuest, in 2001 and today travels the world to speak, consult, and inspire leaders and people everywhere. From 2001-2008, he spent six months a year in Africa and still enjoys visiting and working on that continent where he is now focusing most of his efforts with his ministry partners in Kenya. John is currently a part-time instructor for Ottawa University in Kansas where he teaches theology and leadership classes.

John is a prolific writer and has published many dozens of books—including a verse-by-verse commentary covering the entire New Testament—as well as numerous articles for publications around the world. He serves as a creative and life purpose coach for people in many nations, and his daily and weekly blog posts have a large following, as does his work on other social media outlets. He is currently working on an Old Testament commentary called the Purpose Study Bible.

John has been married since 1974 to Kathryn Stanko, and they have two adult children and two grandchildren. In 2014, John founded Urban Press, a publishing service designed to tell stories of the city, from the city, and to the city through which he serves a diverse community of authors.

Keep in Touch
with John Stanko

Twitter: @John_Stanko
Instagram: stanko.john
Facebook: john.stanko1
LinkedIn: https://www.linkedin.com/in/john-stanko-1600506/

www.purposequest.com
www.johnstanko.us
www.stankobiblestudy.com
www.stankomondaymemo.com

or via email at johnstanko@gmail.com

John also does extensive relief and community development work in Kenya.
You can see some of his projects at:
www.purposequest.com/donate

PurposeQuest International
PO Box 8882
Pittsburgh, PA 15221-0882

And download John's free mobile app, PurposeQuest International,
from Google Play, Amazon Appstore, or the Apple Store

Additional Titles by John Stanko

A Daily Dose of Proverbs

A Daily Taste of Proverbs

Cambiando la Manera en que Hacemos Iglesia

Changing the Way We Do Church, 2nd Edition

Come Adore Him

Go And Obey

I Wrote This Book on Purpose, 2nd Edition

La Vida es una Mina de Oro: Puedes Cavarla?

Life Is A Gold Mine: Can You Dig It? 20th Anniversary Edition

My Enemies, My Friends

Out With the Old, In With the New

Purpose Study Bible: Genesis

Purpose Study Bible: Exodus

Put Me In Coach

Strictly Business

The Leadership Walk

The Power of Purple

The Price of Leadership

Unlocking the Power of Your Creativity

Unlocking the Power of Your Faith

Unlocking the Power of Your Productivity

Unlocking the Power of Your Purpose

Unlocking the Power of Your Thinking

Unlocking the Power of You

Ven a Adorarlo

What Would Jesus Ask You Today?

Your Life Matters

Made in the USA
Middletown, DE
17 May 2022

65834403R00124